Alexander Craig Gibson

The Folk-Speech of Cumberland and some Districts Adjacent

Being Short Stories and Rhymes in the Dialects of the West Border Counties

Alexander Craig Gibson

The Folk-Speech of Cumberland and some Districts Adjacent
Being Short Stories and Rhymes in the Dialects of the West Border Counties

ISBN/EAN: 9783744768184

Printed in Europe, USA, Canada, Australia, Japan

Cover: Foto ©Thomas Meinert / pixelio.de

More available books at **www.hansebooks.com**

THE
Folk-Speech of Cumb[erland]

AND SOME DISTRICTS A[DJACENT]

BEING

SHORT STORIES AND R[HYMES]

IN THE DIALECTS OF THE W[EST]
BORDER COUNTIES.

BY

ALEXANDER CRAIG GIBSON

> What hempen Home-spuns have we swaggering [here?]
> *A Midsummer [Night's Dream.]*
> Speech, manners, morals, all without di[sguise.]

THIRD THOUSAND.

LONDON: JOHN RUSSELL SMITH.
CARLISLE: G. & T. COWARD.
MDCCCLXXIII.

TO

WILLIAM DICKINSON,

OF NORTH MOSSES AND THORNCROFT,

F. L. S.,

Author of "A Glossary of Cumberland Words and Phrases," "Lamplugh Club," "A Prize Essay on the Agriculture of Cumberland," "The Botany of Cumberland," &c., &c., &c.,

THIS VOLUME IS INSCRIBED,

IN CORDIAL RECOGNITION OF
THE PRE-EMINENT INDUSTRY AND SKILL DISPLAYED
IN HIS ELUCIDATIONS OF THE HOMELY SPEECH
OF OUR NATIVE COUNTY,
AND IN
GRATEFUL ACKNOWLEDGEMENT OF THE
UNFAILING SYMPATHY AND THE KINDLY HELP WITH
WHICH HE HAS BRIGHTENED A
FRIENDSHIP OF MANY
YEARS.

PREFACE TO THE FIRST EDITION.

One or two of the Cumberland stories included in this volume, as well as some of the pieces in rhyme, have already been circulated very largely in newspapers, pamphlets, and collections. Their reappearance, along with many hitherto unpublished additions, in this aggregated form, is due mainly to the popularity attained by them separately. Whether they may be as popular in this more pretentious guise as in their humbler, and perhaps, more appropriate form, remains to be tried.

I claim superiority over most of the earlier workers in the same philological ground in respect of the greater purity of my dialect. The Cumberland speech as written herein is pure Cumbrian, as the speech of the Scottish pieces, introduced for variety's sake, is pure Scotch. Miss Blamire, Stagg, Anderson, Rayson, and others, have all written their dialect pieces, more or less, in the *Scoto*-Cumbrian which prevails along the southern side of the west Border. In other respects my inferiority to those deservedly popular writers is sufficiently evident. But, as expositions of the folk-speech of those parts of the County where, and where only, the unadulterated old Norse-rooted Cumbrian vernacular is spoken, I claim for these Tales and Rhymes the distinction of surpassing all similar productions, excepting only the dialect writings of my friend Mr. Dickinson, and perhaps the *Borrowdale Letter* of Isaac Ritson, and the *Gwordie and Will* of Charles Graham. I should not omit to state however, that Mr. John Christian of London, and a writer who assumed the *nom de plume* of Jack Todd, have evinced in their contributions to the local press, a mastery over the dialect of Whitehaven and its vicinity which makes us wish that their pens had been more prolific.

For the illustrations I have attempted of the speech of High Furness and its Westmorland border, I ask no such distinction. The dialect there, as in the adjacent parts of Cumberland, is vitiated by an intermixture of that of the County Palatine, of which Furness forms a portion; and as it is spoken, so, if written at all, should it be written. These appear here for the reason already assigned for the introduction of the Rhymes given in the dialect of Dumfriesshire.

The work rests its claims to favourable consideration entirely on its value as a faithfully rendered contribution to the dialect literature of the country. No higher estimate is sought for it. The production of its various contents has been an occasional amusement indulged in during some of the intervals of leisure and repose afforded by pursuits of a more important, more engrossing, and it is hoped, a more useful character, with which, had it in any wise interfered, it had not been proceeded with. Its composition has been a relaxation, not a task; a divertisement, not an occupation; and had its success when published been deemed incompatible with these conditions, it had not appeared.

BEBINGTON,
December 18th, 1868.

CONTENTS.

		PAGE
Joe and the Geologist	(Cumberland)	1
T' Reets on't	(Ibid.)	6
Bobby Banks' Bodderment	(Ibid.)	15
Wise Wiff	(Ibid.)	23
Lal Dinah Grayson	(Ibid.)	31
Jwohnny, git oot !	(Ibid.)	34
The Runaway Wedding	(Ibid.)	36
Billy Watson' Lonning	(Ibid.)	39
Lone and Weary	(Ibid.)	42
T' Clean Ned o' Kes'ick	(Ibid.)	44
Ben Wells	(Ibid.)	48
Sannter Bella	(Ibid.)	51
Branthet Neùk Boggle	(Ibid.)	54
Mary Ray and Me	(Ibid.)	63

		PAGE
The Bannasyde Cairns	(High Furness)	66
Betty Yewdale	(Ibid.)	71
The Skulls of Calgarth	(Westmorland)	76
Măp'ment	(High Furness)	86
Oxenfell Dobby	(Ibid.)	89
Meenie Bell	(Dumfriesshire)	96
A Lockerbye Lycke	(Old Scotch)	99
The Farmers' Wives o' Annandale	(Dumfriesshire)	109
A Reminiscence of Corrie	(Ibid.)	112
Reminiscences of Lockerbie	(Ibid.)	122
Yan o' t' Elect	(Cumberland)	129
Keàtie Curbison's Cat	(Ibid.)	134
Joseph Thompson's Thumb	(Ibid.)	137
Cursty Benn	(Ibid.)	145
Tom Railton's White Spats	(Ibid.)	148
A Sneck Posset	(Ibid.)	154
Remarks on the Cumberland Dialect		157
Glossary		163

JOE AND THE GEOLOGIST.

A het foorneun, when we war oa' gaily thrang at heàm, an oald gentleman mak' of a fellow com' in tul ooar foald an' said, whyte nateral, 'at he wantit somebody to gà wid him on't fells. We oa' stopt an' teuk a gud leuk at him afoor anybody spak; at last fadder said, middlin' sharp-like—(he ola's speaks that way when we're owte sa thrang, does fadder)—"We've summat else to deu here nor to gà rakin ower t'fells iv a fine day like this, wid nèabody kens whoa." T'gentleman was a queerish like oald chap, wid a sharp leuk oot, grey hair and a smo' feàce—drist i' black, wid a white neckcloth like a parson, an' a par of specks on t'top of a gay lang nwose at wasn't set varra fair atween t' e'en on him, sooa 'at when he leuk't ebbem at yan through his specks he rayder turn't his feàce to t'ya side. He leuk't that way at fadder, gev a lal chèarful bit of a laugh an' said, iv his oan mak' o' toke, 'at he dudn't want to hinder wark, but he wad give anybody 'at ken't t'fells weel, a matter o' five shillin' to gà wid him, an' carry two lāl bags. "Howay wid tha, Joe," sez fadder to me, "it's a croon mair nor iver thoo was wūrth at heàm!" I meàd nèa words aboot it, but gat me-sel' a gud lūmp of a stick, an' away we set, t' oald lang nwos't man an' me, ebbem up t' deàl.

As we war' climmin' t'fell breist, he geh me two empty bags to carry, meàd o' ledder. Thinks I to me-sel', "I's gān to eddle me five shillin' middlin' cannily." I niver thowte he wad finnd owte on t' fells to full his lal bags wid, but I was misteàn!

He turn't oot to be a far lisher oald chap nor a body wad ha' thowte, to leuk at his gray hair and his white hankecher an' his specks. He went lowpin owre wet spots an' gūrt steàns, an' scrafflin across craggs an' screes, tul yan wad ha' sworn he was sūmmat a kin tul a Herdwick tip.

Efter a while he begon leukin' hard at oa't' steàns an' craggs we com' at, an' than he teuk till breckan lūmps off them wid a queer lal hammer he hed wid him, an' stuffin t' bits intil t' bags 'at he geh me to carry. He fairly cap't me noo. I dudn't ken what to mak o' sec a customer as t'is! At last I cudn't help axin him what meàd him cum sèa far up on t'fell to lait bits o' steàns when he may'd finnd sèa many doon i't' deàls? He laugh't a gay bit, an' than went on knappin' away wid his lal hammer, an' said he was a jolly jist. Thinks I to me-sel, thou's a jolly jackass, but it maks nèa matter to me if thou no'but pays me t' five shillin' thou promish't ma.

Varra weel, he keep't on at this feckless wark tul gaily leàt at on i't' efter-neun, an' be that time o' day he'd pang't beàth o't' ledder pwokes as full as they wad hod wid bits o' steàn.

I've nit sèa offen hed a harder darrak efter t' sheep, owther at clippin time or soavin time, as I hed followin' that oald grey heidit chap an' carryin' his ledder bags. But hooiver, we gat back tul oor house afoor neeght. Mūdder gev t' oald jolly jist, as he co't his-sel', some breid an' milk, an' efter he'd teàn that an' toak't a lal bit wid fadder aboot sheep farming an' sec like, he pait ma me five shillin' like a man, an' than tel't ma he wad gi' ma ūdder five shillin' if I wad bring his pwokes full o' steàns doon to Skeàl-hill be nine o'clock i't' mwornin'.

He set off to woak to Skeàl-hill just as it was growin' dark; an' neist mwornin', as seun as I'd gitten me poddish, I teuk t' seàm rwoad wid his ledder bags, ower me shoolder, thinkin' tul me-sel' 'at yan may'd mak a lal fortune oot o' thūr jolly jists if a lock mair on them wad no'but come oor way.

It was anūdder het mwornin', an' I hedn't woak't far till I begon to think that I was as gūrt a feul as t'oald jolly jist to carry brocken steàns o't' way to Skeàl-hill, when I may'd finnd plenty iv any rwoad side, clwose to t' spot I was tackin' them tul. Sooa I shack't them oot o' t' pwokes, an' than stept on a gay bit leeter widout them.

When I com nār to Skeàl-hill, I fūnd oald Aberram Atchisson sittin on a steul breckan steàns to mend rwoads wid, an' I ax't him if I med full my ledder pwokes frae his heap. Aberram was varra kaim't' an' tell't ma to tak them 'at wasn't brocken if I wantit steàns, sooa I tell't him hoo it was an' oa' aboot it. T' oald maizlin was like to toytle of his steul wid laughin', an' said me mūdder sud tak gud care on ma, for I was ower sharp a chap to leeve varra lang i' this warld; but I'd better full my pwokes as I liked, an' mak' on wid them.

T' jolly jist hed just gitten his breakfast when I gat to Skeàl-hill, an' they teuk ma intil t' parlour tul him. He gūrned oa't feàce ower when I went in wid his bags, an' tell't me to set them doon in a neuk, an' than ax't ma if I wad hev some breakfast. I said I'd gitten me poddish, but I dudn't mind; sooa he tell't them to bring in some mair coffee, an' eggs, an' ham, an' twoastit breid an' stuff, an' I gat sec a breakfast as I niver seed i' my time, while t' oald gentleman was gittin' his-sel' rūddy to gang off in a carriage 'at was waitin' at t' dooar for him.

When he com doon stairs he geh me t'udder five shillin' an' pait for my breakfast an' what he'd gitten his-sel. Than he tell't me to put t' ledder bags wid t' steàns in them on beside t' driver's feet, an' in he gat, an' laugh't an' noddit, an' away he went.

I niver owder seed nor heard mair of t' oald jolly jist, but I've offen thowte ther mun be parlish few steàns i' his country, when he was sooa pleas't at gittin' two lāl ledder bags full for ten shillin', an' sec a breakfast as that an'. It wad be a faymish job if fadder could sell o' t' steàns iv oor fell at five shillin' a pwokeful—wadn't it ?

T' REETS ON'T;

BEING

Another Supplement to "Joe and the Geologist."

BY JOE HIS-SEL'.

"A supplement to Joe and the Geologist, by another hand," appeared some time ago, in the *Whitehaven Herald*, and was afterwards published as a pamphlet. Joe, is represented therein as giving to a comrade called Tommy Towman, an account of his second meeting with the Geologist, and making himself seem conscious of having played an ugly trick, and appealing to his old friend's clemency on the ground that his father was dead; and thinking his character misconstrued, of course unintentionally, here gives "T' Reets on't."

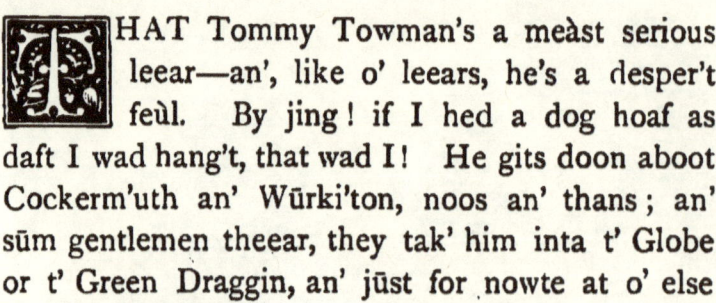HAT Tommy Towman's a meàst serious leear—an', like o' leears, he's a desper't feùl. By jing! if I hed a dog hoaf as daft I wad hang't, that wad I! He gits doon aboot Cockerm'uth an' Wŭrki'ton, noos an' thans; an' sŭm gentlemen theear, they tak' him inta t' Globe or t' Green Draggin, an' jŭst for nowte at o' else

but acoase they think he kens me, they feed him wid drink an' they hod him i' toak till he can hardly tell whedder end on him's upbank; an' than they dro' him on to tell them o' mak's o' teàls—o' mak's but true an's—aboot me; an' t' pooar lāl gowk hesn't gumption aneuf to see 'at they're no'but makin' ghem on him. But, loavin' surs! if he'd hed t' sense of a gūrse gā'n gezlin he wad niver ha' browte oot sec a lafter o' lees as he's gitten yan o' them Wūrki'ton gentlemen (yan 'at ken's weel hoo to write doon oor heàmly toke) to put inta prent; an' what mak's yan madder nor o' t' rest,—to put them i' prent jūst as if I'd tel't them me-sel'. I's nūt t' chap to try to cum ower an oald jolly jist wid whinin' oot "Fadder's deid!" when ivery body kens 'at fadder's whicker nor meàst on us. My sarty! he's nin o' t' deein' mak' isn't fadder. We s' hev to wūrry fadder when his time cūms, for he'll niver dee of his-sel' sa lang as ther's any wark to hoond yan on tull. An' I needn't tell any body 'at knows *me*, 'at I was niver t' chap to tak' in owder a jolly jist or any udder feùl; an' if I was, I's nūt a likely fellow to be freeten't for what I'd done. But ther's m'appen sūm 'at doesn't; an' mebbee ther's a lock 'at doesn't know what a leear Tommy Towman is, an' sooa, bee t' way o' settin' me-sel' reet wid beath maks, I'll tell yé what *dūd* gā forret 'atween me an' t' jolly jist t' seckint time he com tul Skeàl-hill.

I said afooar 'at I'd niver seen mair o' t' oald jolly jist, an' when I said that, I hedn't; but yā donky neet last summer fadder hed been doon Lorton way, an' 't was gaily leàt when he gat heàm. As he was sittin' iv his oàn side o' t' fire, tryin' to lowse t' buttons of his spats, he says to me, "Joe," says he, "I co't at Skeàl-hill i' my rwoad heàm." Mudder was sittin' knittin' varra fast at hūr side o' t' hārth; she hedn't oppen't her mooth sen fadder co' heàm, —nay, she hedn't sa mūch as leuk't at him efter t' ya hard glowre 'at she gev him at t' fūrst; but when he said he'd been at Skeàl-hill, she gev a grunt, an' said, as if she spak till nèabody but hur-sel', "Ey! a blinnd body med see that." "I was speakin' till Joe," says fadder. "Joe," says he, "I was at Skeàl-hill"—anudder grunt—"an' they tel't me 'at thy oald frind t' jolly jist's back ageàn—I think thu'd better slip doon an' see if he wants to buy any mair brocken steàns; oald Aberram hes a fine heap or two liggin aside Kirgat. An', noo, 'at I've gitten them spats off, I's away to my bed." Mudder tok a partin' shot at him as he stacker't off. She said, "It wad be as weel for sūm on us if yé wad bide theear, if yé mean to carry on i' t' way ye're shappin'!" Noo, this was hardly fair o' mudder, for it's no'but yance iv a way 'at fadder cū's heàm leàt an' stackery; but I wasn't sworry to see him git a lāl snape, he's sae rūddy wid his snapes his-sel'. I ken't weel aneuf he was no'but mackin' ghem o' me aboot gittin' mair brass oot o't' oald jolly jist, but I thowte to me-sel', thinks I, I've deun many a dafter thing nor tak' him at his wūrd, whedder he meen't it or nūt, an' sooa thowte, sooa deùn; for neist mworning' I woak't me-sel' off tull Skeàl-hill.

When I gat theear, an' as't if t' jolly jist was sturrin', they yan snùrtit an' anudder gurn't, till I gat rayder maddish; but at last yan o' them skipjacks o' fellows 'at ye see weearin' a lāl jacket like a lass's bedgoon, sed he wad see. He com back laughin', an' said, "Cūm this way, Joe." Well, I follow't him till he stopp't at a room dooar, an' he gev a lal knock, an' than oppen't it, an' says, "Joe, sur," says he. I wasn't gā'n to stand that, ye know, an' says I, "Joe, sur," says I, "he'll ken it's Joe, sur," says I, "as seùn as he sees t' feàce o' me;" says I, "an' if thoo doesn't git oot o' that wid thy 'Joe sur,'" says I, "I'll fetch the' a clink under t' lug 'at 'll mak' the' laugh at t' wrang side o' that ugly mug o' thine, thoo gūrnin yap, thoo!" Wid that he skipt oot o't' way gaily sharp, an' I stept whietly into t' room. Theear he was, sittin at a teàble writin—t' grey hair, t' specks, t' lang nwose, t' white hankecher, an' t' black cleàs, o' just as if he'd niver owder doff't his-sel' or donn't his-sel' sen he went away. But afooar I cūd put oot my hand or say a civil wūrd tull him, he glentit up at mé throo his specks, iv his oan oald sideways fashion—but varra feùrce-like—an' grūntit oot sum'at aboot

wūnderin' hoo I dār't to shew my feàce theear.
Well! this pot t' cap on t' top of o'. I'd chow't
ower what fadder said, an' *hoo* he'd said it i' my
rwoad doon, till I fūnd me-sel' gittin rayder mad
aboot that. T' way 'at they snurtit an' laugh't
when I com to Skeàl-hill meàd me madder; an' t'
bedgoon cwoatit fellow wid his "Joe, sur," meàd
me madder nor iver; but t' oald jolly jist, 'at I
thowte wad be sa fain to see mé ageàn, if 't hed
no'but been for t' seàk of oor sprogue on t' fells
togidder—wùnderin' 'at I dar't show my feàce
theear, fairly dreàv me *rantin'* mad, an' I *dūd* mak
a brūst.

"Show my feàce!" says I, "an' what sùd I show
than?" says I. "If it cūms to showin' feàces, I've
a better feàce to show nor iver belang't to yan o'
your breed," says I, "if t' rest on them's owte like
t' sample they've sent us; but if yé mūn know, I's
cūm't of a stock 'at niver wad be freetn't to show a
feàce till a king, let aleàn an oald newdles wid a
creùkt nwose, 'at co's his-sel' a jolly jist: an' I defy
t' feàce o' clay," says I, " to say 'at any on us iver
dūd owte we need shām on whoariver we show't
oor feàces. Dār to show my feàce, eh?" says I,
" my song! but this is a bonnie welcome to give a
fellow 'at's cum't sa far to see yé i' seckan a
mwornin'!" I said a gay deal mair o' t' seàm
mak', an' o' t' while I was sayin' on't—or, I sūd say,
o' t' while I was shootin' on't, for I dudn't spar' t'

noise—t' oald thief laid his-sel' back iv his girt chair, an' keept twiddlin' his thooms an' glimin' ūp at mé, wid a hoaf smūrk iv his feàce, as if he'd gitten sum'at funny afooar him. Efter a while I stopt, for I'd ron me-sel' varra nār oot o' winnd, an' I begon rayder to think shām o' shootin' an' bellerin' sooa at an oald man, an' him as whisht as a troot throo it o'; an' when I'd poo't in, he just said as whietly as iver, 'at I was a natteral cur'osity. I dùdn't ken weel what this meen't, but I thowte it was soace, an' it hed like to set mé off ageàn, but I beàtt it doon as weel as I cūd, an' I said, "Hev yé gitten owte ageān mé?" says I. "If yé hev, speak it oot like a man, an' divn't sit theear twiddlin yer silly oald thooms an' coa'in fwoke oot o' ther neàms i' that rwoad!" Than it o' com oot plain aneuf. O' this illnater was just acoase I hedn't brong him t' steàns 'at he'd gedder't on t' fells that het day, an' he said 'at changin' on them was ayder a varra dūrty trick or a varra clumsy jwoke. "Trick!" says I. "Jwoke! dud yé say? It was rayder past a jwoke to expect me to carry a leàd o' brocken steàns o' t' way here, when ther' was plenty at t' spot. I's nūt sec a feùl as ye've teàn me for." He tok off his specks, an' he glower't at mé adoot them; an' than he pot them on ageàn, an' glower't at mé wid them; an' than he laugh't an' ax't mé if I thowte ther' cud be nèa difference i' steàns. "Whey," says I, "ye'll hardly hev t' feàce to tell me 'at ya bag o' steàns isn't as gud as anudder bag o' steàns—an' suer*lye* to man, ye'll niver be sa consaitit as to say yé can break steàns better nor oald Aberram 'at breaks them for his breid, an' breaks them o' day lang, an' ivery day?" Wid that he laugh't agean an' tel't mé to sit doon, an' than ax't me what I thowte meàd him tak so mickle trùble laitin' bits o' stean on t' fells if he cud git what he wantit at t' rwoad side. "Well!" says I, "if I mun tell yé t' truth, I thowte yé war rayder nick't i' t' heid; but it meàd nea matter what I thowte sa lang as yé pait mé sa weel for gān wid yé." As I said this, it com into my heid 'at it's better to flaitch a feùl nor to feight wid him; an' efter o', 'at ther' may'd be sum'at i't' oald man likin steans of his oan breakin' better nor ùdder fwoke's. I remember't t' fiddle 'at Dan Fisher meàd, an' 'at he thowte, his-sel', was t' best fiddle 'at iver squeak't, for o' it meàd ivery body else badly to hear't; an' wad bray oald Ben Wales at his dancing scheùl boal acoase Ben wadn't play t' heàm meàd fiddle asteed of his oan. We o' think meàst o' what we've hed a hand in oorsel's—it's no'but natteral; an' sooa as o' this ron throo my heid, I fūnd me-sel' gitten rayder sworry for t' oald man, an' I says, "What wad yé gi' me to git yé o' yer oan bits o' steàn back ageàn?" He cockt up his lugs at this, an' ax't mé if his speciments, as he co't them, was seaf. "Ey," says I, "they're seàf aneùf; neàbody hereaboot 'ill think a lal lock o' steans worth meddlin' on, sa lang as they divn't lig i' the'r rwoad." Wid that he jūmpt ūp an' said I mud hev sum'at to drink. Thinks I to me-sel', Cūm! we're gittin' back to oor oan menseful way ageàn at t' lang last, but I willn't stūr a peg till I ken what I's to hev for gittin him his rubbish back, I wad niver hear t' last on't if I went heàm em'ty handit." He meád it o' reet hooiver, as I was tackin' my drink; an' he went up t' stair an' brong doon t' ledder bags I kent sa weel, an' geh mé them to carry just as if nowte hed happen't, an' off we startit varra like as we dūd afooar.

T' Skeàl-hill fwoke o' gedder't aboot t' dooar to leùk efter us, as if we'd been a show. We, nowder on us, mindit for that, hooiver, but stump't away togidder as thick as inkle weavers till we gat till t' feùt of oor girt meedow, whoar t' steans was liggin, aside o' t' steel, just as I'd teem't them oot o' t' bags, only rayder grown ower wid gūrse. As I pick't them up, yan by yan, and handit them to t' oald jolly jist, it dūd my heart gūd to see hoo pleas't he leùkt, as he wiped them on his cwoat cūff, an' wettit them, an' glower't at them throo his specks—an' pack't them away into t' bags till they wer' beàth chock full ageàn.

Well! t' bargin was, 'at I sud carry them to Skeàl-hill. Sooa back we pot—t' jolly jist watchin' his bags o't' way as if t' steans was guineas, an' I was a thief. When we gat theear, he meàd mé tak' them reet into t' parlour; an' t' fūrst thing he dūd was to co' for sum reed wax an' a leet, an' clap a greet splatch of a seal on t' top of ayder bag; an' than he leùkt at me, an' gev a lal grunt of a laugh, an' a smartish wag of his heid, as much as to say, "Dee it agean, if thoo can, Joe!" But efter that he says, "Here, Joe," says he, "here five shillin' for restworin' my speciments, an' here anudder five shillin' for showin' mé a speciment of human natur' 'at I didn't believe in till to-day." Wid that, we shak't hands an' we partit; an' I went heàm as pleas't as a dog wi' two tails, jinglin' my mūnny an' finndin' sūm way as if I was hoaf a jolly jist me-sel'. When I gat theear, I says to fadder, "Fadder," says I, "leùk yé here! If o' yer jibes turn't to sec as this, I divn't mind if ye jibe on till yé've jibed yer-sel' intul a tip's whorn;" says I, "but I reckon yé niver jibed to sec an' end for yer-sel' as ye've jibed for me this time!"

BOBBY BANKS' BODDERMENT.

(A Sup of Coald Keàl het up ageàn.)

HE was ola's a top marketer was ooar Betty, she niver miss't gittin' t' best price gā'n beàth for butter an' eggs; an' she ken't hoo to bring t' ho'pennies heàm! Nūt like t' meàst o' fellows' wives 'at thinks there's nèa hūrt i' warin' t' odd brass iv a pictur' beuk or gūd stūff for t' barnes, or m'appen sūm'at whyte as needless for the'rsels,—Betty ola's brong t' ho'pennies heàm.

Cockerm'uth's ooar reg'lar market—it's a gay bit t' bainer—but at t' time o' year when Kes'ick's full o' quality ther's better prices to be gitten theear; an' sooa o' through t' harvest time, an' leater on, she ola's went to Kes'ick. Last back-end, hooiver, Betty was fash'd sadly wid rheumatics iv her back, an' yā week she cūd hardly git aboot at o', let alean gā to t' market. For a while she wadn't mak ūp her mind whedder to send me iv her spot, or ooar.

eldest dowter, Faith; but as Faith was hardly fowerteen—stiddy aneuf of her yeàge, but *rayder* yŭng,—Betty thowte she'd better keep Faith at heàm an' let me tak' t' marketin' to Kes'ick.

Of t' Setterda' mwornin', when it com', she hed us o' ŭp an' stŭrrin', seùner nor sŭm on us liket; an' when I'd gitten sŭm'at to eat, iv a hŭgger mŭgger mak' of a way, says Betty till me, says she— "Here's six an' twenty pŭnd o' butter," says she. "If thoo was gud for owte thoo wad git a shilling a pŭnd for't ivery slake. Here's five dozen of eggs," says she, "*I* wadn't give a skell o' them mair nor ten for sixpence," says she, "but *thoo* mun git what thoo can," says she, "efter thu's fŭnd oot what ŭdder fwoke's axin. When thu's meàd thy market," says Betty, "thu'll gā to t' draper's an' git me a yard o' check for a brat, a knot o' tape for strings tŭl't, an' a hank o' threed to sowe't wid—if I's gud for nowte else, I can *sowe* yit," says she, wid a gurn; "than thoo mŭn git hoaf a pŭnd o' tea an' a quarter of a steàn o' sugger—they ken my price at Crosstet's—an' hoaf a steàn o' soat, an' a pŭnd o' seàp, an' hoaf a pŭnd o' starch, an' a penn'orth o' steàn-blue, an' git me a bottle o' that stuff to rŭb my back wid; an' than thoo ma' git two oonces o' 'bacca for thysel'.

If thoo leùks hoaf as sharp as thoo sŭd leùk thu'll be through wid beàth thy marketin' an' thy shoppin' by twelve o'clock; an' thoo ma' gā an' git a bit o' dinner, like ūdder fwoke, at Mistress Boo's, an' a pint o' yall. Efter that t' seùner thoo starts for heàm an' t' better. Noo thu'll mind an' forgit nowte? Ther' t' check, an' t' tape, an' t' threed, that's three things—t' tea, an' t' sugger, an' t' soat, an' t' seàp, an' t' starch, an' t' steàn-blue, an' t' rūbbin' stūff, an' t' 'bacca—I's up-ho'd the' nūt to forgit that!—elebben. Ten things for me, an' yan for thysel'! I *think* I've meàd o' plain aneùf; an' noo, if thoo misses owte I'll say thoo's a bigger clot-heid nor I've teàn the' for—an' that 'ill be sayin' nèa lal!"

Many a fellow wad tak t' 'frunts if his wife spak till him i' that way—but bliss yè I've leev't lang aneùf wid Betty to know 'at it's no'but a way she hes o' shewin' her likin'. When she wants to be t' kindest an' best to yan, yan's ola's suer to git t' warst wūrd 'at she can finnd i' t' inside on her!

Well, I set off i' gūd fettle for Kes'ick, gat theear i' gradely time, an' pot ūp at Mistress Boo's. I hed a sharpish market, an' seùn gat shot o' my būtter an' eggs at better prices nor Betty toak't on. I bowte o' t' things at she wantit, an' t' 'bacca for mysel', an' gat a gud dinner at Mistress Boo's, an' a pint o' yall an' a crack.

He wad be a cliverish fellow 'at went ta Kes'ick an' gat oot on't adoot rain; an' suer aneùf, by t' time 'at I'd finished my pint and my crack, it was cūmmin' doon as it knows hoo to cūm doon at Kes'ick.

But when it rains theear, they hev to deù as they deù ūnder Skiddaw, *let it fo!* an' wet or dry, I hed to git heàm tūll Betty.

When I was aboot startin', I begon to think ther' was sum'at mair to tak wid me. I coontit t' things ower i' my basket hoaf a dozen times. Theear they o' warr—ten for Betty, yan for me! Than what the dang-ment was't I was forgittin? I was suer it was sūm'at, but for t' heart on me I cūdn't think what it med be. Efter considerin' for a lang time, an' gittin' anūdder pint to help mé to consider, I set off i' t' rain wid my basket an' t' things in't, anonder my top-sark to keep o' dry.

Bee t' time I gat to Portinskeàl, I'd begon to tire! T' wedder was slattery, t' rwoads was slashy, t' basket was heavy, an' t' top sark meàd me het; but t' thowtes o' hevin' forgitten sūm'at tew't mè t' warst of o'. I rūstit theear a bit—gat anudder pint, an' coontit my things ower and ower, "Ten for Betty!—yan for my-sel." I cūd mak nowder mair nor less on them. Cockswūnters!—what hed I forgitten? Or what was't 'at meàd mè suer I'd forgitten sūm'at when I'd o' t' things wid mè?

I teuk t' rwoad agean mair nor hoaf crazy.

I stop't ūnder a tree aside Springbank, an' Dr.—— com' ridin' up through t' rain, on his black galloway. "Why, Robert," says he, "ye look as if ye'd lost something." "Nay, doctor," says I, "here t' check an' t' tape an' t' threed—I' lost nowte—that's three.

Here t' soat, an' t' seàp, an' t' starch, an' t' steànblue—that's sebben—I' lost nowte, but I' forgitten sum'at. Here t' tea, an' t' sugger, an' t' rūbbin' bottle—that's ten; an' here t' 'bacca—that's elebben. —Ten for Betty, an' yan for me! Ten for Betty, an' yan for me!! Doctor, doctor," says I, "fwoke say ye ken oa things—what *hev* I forgitten?" "I'll tell ye what ye haven't forgotten," says he, "ye haven't forgotten the ale at Keswick. Get home, Robert, get home," says he, "and go to bed and sleep it off." I believe he thowte I was drūnk; but I wasn't—I was no'but maizelt wid tryin' to finnd oot what I'd forgitten.

As I com nār to t' Swan wid two Necks I fell in wid greet Gweordie Howe, and says I, "Gweordie my lad," says I, "I's straddelt," says I, "I's fairly maiz't," says I. "I left sūm'at ahint me at Kes'ick, an' I've thowte aboot it till my heid's gā'n like a jobjūrnal," says I, "an' what it is *I* cannot tell." "Can t'e nūt?" says Gweordie. "Can t'e nūt? Whey, than, cūm in an' see if a pint o' yall 'll help thé'." Well, I steud pints, an' Gweordie steud pints, an' I steud pints ageàn. Anūdder time I wad ha' been thinkin' aboot what Betty wad say till o' this pintin', but I was gittin' despert aboot what I'd forgitten at Kes'ick, an' I cūd think o' nowte else.

T' yall was gud aneùf, but it dùdn't kest a morsel o' leet on what was bodderin' on ma sa sair, an' I teuk t' rwoad ageàn finndin' as if I was farder off 't nor iver.

T' rain keep't cūmmin' doon—t' rwoad gat softer an' softer—t' basket gat heavier an' heavier—t' top sark hetter an' hetter, an' my heid queerer an' queerer. If I stopt anonder ya tree i' t' wūd, I stopt anonder twenty, an' coontit ower t' things i' t' basket till they begon to shap' theirsels intil o' mak's o' barnish sangs i' my heid, and I fūnd mysel' creunin' away at sec bits of rhymes as thūrr—

> Ten things an' yan, Bobby,
> Ten things an' yan ;
> Here five an' five for Betty Banks,
> An' yan for Betty's man.

"Lord preserve oor wits—sec as they ūrr," says I. "I mūn be gā'n wrang i' my heid when I've teān till mackin' sangs!" But t' queerest break was 'at I dūddn't mak' them—they meàd thersel's—an' they meàd me sing them an' o', whedder I wad or nūt—an' off I went ageàn till a different teùn—

> Says Betty—says she ; says Betty till me—
> "If owte thoo contrives to forgit,
> "I'll reckon thè' daìzter an' dafter," says she,
> "Nor iver I've reckon't thè' yit."
> I's daizter an' dafter nor iver, she'll say,
> An' marry, she willn't say wrang !
> But scold as she will, ey, an' gūrn as she may,
> I'll sing her a bonnie lāl sang, lāl sang,
> I'll sing her a bonnie lāl sang.

"Well ! It hes cūm't till whoa wad hae thowte it," says I, "if I cannot stop mysel' frae mackin' sangs an' singin' them of a wet day i' Widdup Wūd ; I'll coont t' things ower ageàn," says I, "an' see if that'll stop ma." Ye ma' believe ma or nūt, as ye like, but iv anūdder tick-tack there was I coontin' t' things ower iv a sang :—

> Here t' check an' t' tape an' t' threed, oald lad!
> Here t' soat an' t' sugger an' t' tea—
> Seàp, starch, steàn-blue, an' t' bottle to rub,
> An' t' 'bacca by 'tsel' on't for me,
> Here t' 'bacca by 'tsel' on't for me, me, me,
> Here t' 'bacca by 'tsel' on't for me.
> I'll niver git heàm while Bobby's my neàm,
> But maffle an' sing till I dee, dee, dee,
> But maffle an' sing till I dee!

"Weel, weel," says I, "if I *is* oot o' my senses—I IS oot o' my senses, an' that's oa' aboot it,—but

> Loavins what'll Betty think, Betty think, Betty think,
> Loavins what'll Betty think if Bobby bide away?
> She'll sweer he's warin' t' brass i' drink, t' brass i' drink, t' brass i' drink,
> She'll sweer he's warin' t' brass i' drink this varra market-day.
> She's thrimlin' for her būtter-brass, her būtter-brass, her būtter-brass,
> She's thrimlin' for her būtter brass, but willn't thrimle lang.
> For Bobby lad thū's hūr to feàce, thū's hūr to feàce, thū's hur to feàce,
> For Bobby lad, thū's hūr to feàce; she'll m'appen change thy sang.

Sang or nèa sang, t' thowtes o' hevin' "hūr to feàce," an' that gaily seùn, rayder brong me to my oan oald sel' ageàn. I set off yance mair, an' this time, I dūdn't stop while I gat fairly into t' foald.

Faith seed me cūmmin', an' met me ootside o' t' hoose dooar, an' says Faith, "Whoar t' meear an' t' car, fadder?" I dropp't my basket, an' I geàp't at her! Lal Jacop com runnin oot, an' says Jacop, "Fadder, whoar t' meear an' t' car?" I swattit mysel' doon on t' stean binch, an' I glower't at them—furst at yan an' than at t' tudder on them. Betty com limpin' by t' God-speed, an' says Betty, "What hes t'e meàd o' t' car an' t' meear, thoo maizlin?" I gat my speech ageàn when Betty spak', an', hoaf crazet an' hoaf cryin', I shootit oot, "'Od's wūns an' deeth, that's what I' forgitten!" That was what *I* said. What *Betty* said I think I willn't tell yè.

WISE WIFF.

IT was a fine job for Wilfrid Wankelthet 'at his fadder was bworn afooar him. If he'd cùm't into t' warld pooar, he wad ha' bidden pooar, an' geàn pooarer an' pooarer still, till he'd finish't on t' parish.

He was yan o' t' hafe-rock't mack, was Wiffy, varra làl in him but what was putten in wid a speùn, an' that hed run a gay deal mair to body nor brains.

For o' that he wasn't a bad fellow, an' he wasn't badly thowte on. Many a body said o' Wise Wiff, 'at if he hedn't mūch in him, t' làl he hed in him wasn't of a bad pattren; an' es for his manishment, if he'd nò'but stuck till his fadder' advice, he needn't ha' gitten sa varra far wrang.

T' way he gat his fadder's advice was this. When t' oald man fund 'at he was gà'n whoar he cūdn't carry his land an' his morgidges, an' his mūnney, an' his moiderment alang wid him—whoar they wadn't dee him mickle gūd if he cūd—he sent for Jobby Jinkison, o' Jūrtinsyke, a smo' farmer of his 'at hed deùn a gūd deal o' bisness for him at fairs, an' markets, an' seàles, an' sec like, efter he'd growne ower frail to git fray heàm his-sel'; an', says he, "Jobby, I's leavin't o'," he says, "I've meàd a fair scraffle, Jobby," says he, "an' I've gedder't a gay bit togidder, but I can't tack it wid me, Jobby, an' I's wantin to speak till thé' aboot that pooar lad o' mine, 'at it o' hes to cūm till. Nèabody kens better nor thee what he's shwort on—nèabody kens so weel hoo I've triet to git a bit o' edication drūven intūl him, an' hoo lāl we've meàd on't. Ya scheùlmaister said he was shwort o' apprehension; auūdder, 'at he wantit ability; an' a thūrd, 'at he hed nèa capacity. If thùr hed been things 'at mūnny wad ha' bowte, he sūd hed them o', but they warn't. What God's left oot we cannot o' put in, thoo knows, an' we mūn sūbmit—we mūn submit, Jobby," says he, "an' mack t' best o' things as they ūrr. But I cūd sūbmit better—I cūd dee easier if thoo wad promish to leùk efter things for him when I's geàn. I divn't want him to be idle o' togidder, an' sooa I wad wish him to keep t' Booin-leys iv his oan hand—it'll give him sūm'at to think aboot, an' mack fwoke leùk up till him mair nor if he was deùin nowte at o'; an' I fancy 'at if thoo wad agree to deù o' his buyin an' sellin for him, an' seàv him fray bein teán in an' laugh't at, I cūd be happier noo. *Wil*'tè?" Jobby wasn't a man o' many wūrds, but he said "I will, maister! I'll dee o' for him t' seám as if ye war heear to worder it yersel' an' see it deùn. Wid t' farms o' weel set—wid t' Booin-leys liggin i' girse, an' wid me to leùk efter his barg'ins, I wad like to see t' fellow 'at wad laugh at ooar Wiff." "I believe the', Jobby—I believe the', my lad," says t' deein maŋ, "I leùk't for nēa less at thy hand. Fetch him in here, an' I'll tell him afooar the' what I wis' him to deù when I's geàn. Wiffy, my lad," says he, as his son com in, leùken, as he thowte, mair sackless nor iver. "Wiffy, my pooar lad, thy oald fadder's gā'n to leave thee. Whey, whey, gūd lad! it's reet aneùf thoo sūd be sworry to lwoase sec a fadder, but divn't gowl i' that way," for Wiff hed brassen oot wid a meàst terrable rooar. "I say I hev to leave thee, an' that afooar lang. Hod thy noise, thoo bellerin coaf, an' hear what I've to say," says t' fadder, as he got oot o' patience at Wiff's gowlin, an' went back tūll his oald hard way o' speakin til him. "Stop thy beelin, I say, an' lissen to me. I've hed Jobby here browte ower, ebben o' pûrpose, to mack him promish 'at he'll leùk efter thee when I's away. Hod t' noise on the', wil'té! I's leevin the' weel providit for, an' o' t' land mūn be let but t' Booin-leys; thoo mūn keep them i' thy oan hand—thūrty yacre o' gûd grūnd. Ey," says he, hoaf till hissel, "t' best land 'at iver laid oot o' dooars. Whativer way ye gang fray't ye warsen! Thoo'll hod them i' thy oan hand, for t' seàk o' hevin sūm'at to deù. Thoo'll hev to leùk efter t' fences, an' t' yatts, an' t' water-coorses. Keep *them* i' order; an' keep t' plew oot o' t' land; it 'ill give t' meàst liggin t' green side ūp. Jobby 'ill deù thy tradin' for the'. Dūnnot thee mell wid buyin or sellin. Leave o' that to Jobby, an' pay him whativer he charges for his trūble. He'll deù what's reet, will Jobby. An' noo I's aboot deùn. Gi' me yer hands, beàth on yé, an' say ye'll deù what I tell yè. Wilfrid! thoo'll be advised by Jobby. Jobby! thoo'll be true frind to my pooar lad, as if I was theear to see. Promish!"

This was a langish noration for a body wid t' breath leavin him, an' when it was deùn he laid back on his pilliver, an' leùk't at them varra wistful-like, till they promish't, an' it was a bit afooar they cūd, for by this time they war beàth on them yewlin, t' yan ower t' ùdder, whedder to yewl t' hardest.

When t' oald man was bury't oot o' geàt, Wilfrid an' Jobby wūrk't away togidder varra cannily. Job bowte t' stock for t' Booin-leys, an' selt them as they fatten't off, an' enter't o' iv a big beùk 'at Wiff niver so mūch as leùk't atween t' backs on. He'd his fadder's last wūrds for Jobby deein what was reet, an' they war aneùf.

Nowte com to put owder on them oot of his way, till Wiff gat a wife—or mebbe I wad be narder t' truth if I said, a wife gat Wiff—for when ivery body seed 'at he went on i' sec a stiddy soort of a way—gittin heavy incomins i' rent, an' interest, an' shares, an' neábody kent what; an' makin varra leet oot-gangins, it was plain aneùf 'at he wad seùn be yan o' t' yablest men i' thur parts, an' t' lasses begon to cock ther caps at him of o' sides—'specially them 'at thowte a man isn't wūrth hevin if he hesn't a bit o' t' feàce o' t' yūrth; an' efter a while yan o' that mack fassen't Wiffy.

She meàd him a fairish wife, as wives gang, an' if she'd no'but been wise aneùf ta tack him as he was, an' let things gā on as they hed deùn, o' wad been weel; but she cudn't bide t' thowtes of oanin', owder till hersel' or ūdder fwoke, 'at she'd weddit a Tommy Moakison for t' seàk of his brass; an' sooa she keept eggin him on to dee his oan tūrns, an' let fwoke see 'at he wasn't sec a natteral as he was co't. It was this whim-wham o' t' wife's 'at gat him t' nick-neām of Wise Wiff, an' it com tūl him i' this geàt. Amang t' stock ga'n on t' Booin-leys ya year there happen't to be hoaf a scwore of as bonnie Galloway Scots as iver hed yār o' t' ootside on them. Jobby hed bowte them i' t' spring o' t' year at a gūddish price, acoase he seed ther was mūnny to be gitten oot on them efter a sūmmer's rūn iv a gūd pastur'. Jūst as they war rūddy for a cūstomer, an' Wiff was thinkin o' gā'n doon to Jobby to toke aboot sellin on them, t' wife says "There's a butcher cūmmin fray Cockerm'uth to-day aboot buyin them Scots." "Whey thàn," says Wilfrid, "I's just step doon to Jobby, an' tell him to cūm up an' meet t' butcher." "Thoo'll dee nowte o' t' mack," says t' mistress, "Thoo'll set to wark, as a gentlemen sūd dee, an' let Jobby Jinkison, an' ivery body else, see 'at thoo wants néabody to cūm atween thee an' thy oan bisness." "Well, but," says Wiff, "I promish't fadder on his deith-bed 'at Jobby sūd dee o' t' buyin' an' sellin." "Niver thee mind that," says she, "fadder willn't cūm back to claim thee promish, an' if he dūd, I wad tell him 'at if a promish isn't reet it's wrang to keep it. Thoo'll dee as I tell thee." "Well, but," says pooar Wiffy ageàn, "fadder meàd me varra nār sweear tul't." "Shaff o' thee fadder!" says she, "What sense is ther i' flingin a deid fadder iv a leevin wife's feàce i' this ugly fashin. Does t'e know what t' scriptur' says aboot it?—'at a man mūn leave his fadder and mudder, an' stick till his wife! I say ageàn, sell thee oan gūds thee oan sel', an' mack t' best thoo can on them." "But hoo's I to ken what price to ex," says he. "Whey," says she, "cannot thoo leuk into t' beuk 'at Jobby writes o' doon in, an' finnd t' price he pait for them? That'll be a guide for the'. But I wad rayder loase a pūnd or two, if I was thee, nor be meàd a barne on any lang-er." Like many a cliverer fellow, pooar Wiff fūnd ther was nowte for't but lettin his wife hev her way; an' when t' butcher com, he went reet ower wid him to t' fields whoar t' bullocks was gā'n, an' sel't them tūll him oot o' hand.

Iv his rwoạd heàm he went roond by Jūrtinsyke to tell Jobby of his mwornin's wark. Jobby leuk't rayder strūcken iv a heap when he hārd it; but efter considerin a lāl bit, he said, "Weel, maister," (he oalas spack respectful-like to pooar Wilfrid, dūd Jobby his-sel, an' he wadn't let any body else dee udder ways when he was theear.) " Weel, maister," says Jobby, "I willn't oalas be here to mannish for yé, an' yé may as weel begin noo as efter I's geàn to try yer fist at tradin. But what gat ye for t' Scots?" "I dūd bravely, lad," says Wiff, "I dūd bravely. I gat nine pūnd ten a heid for them." "Nine pūnd ten!" Jobby shootit, "Whey, that's what I geh for them mair nor five mūnth sen!" "I ken that," says Wiff, "I teùk a peep into t' girt beùk, an' fūnd theear what thu'd gi'en for them." "An' yé jūst gat what they cost i' t' spring?" says Jobby. "I think if yè carry on a trade like that owte sa lang, ye'll be mackin' t' oald maister's mūnny bags leùk gaily wankle." "Mūnny bags," says Wiff, "What's t' use o' toakin' aboot mūnny bags? T' mūnny bags is seàf aneùf sa lang as I git as mūch for beasts as I *gi'* for them. I think I've meàd a varra fair trade, whativer thoo may think." "Aih dear! aih dear!" says Job, "it wad mack t' oald maister git up oot o' his grave if he cūd hear this. Whoar's t' rent o' t' land to cūm fray wid yer fair trade." "T' rent o' t' land, thoo oald neudles," says Wiff, "t' rent o' what land? T' land's my oan!"

Sooa Mistress Wanklethet fūnd 'at her fadder-in-lo', kent his sūn better nor she dūd her man; an' o' 'at com of her middlin was to git her husband a nickneàm an' mack him a by-würd; for iver sen, when any body theear aboots macks a queerish bargin, somebody else is suer to say, "T' land's my oan, says Wise Wiff!"

LAL DINAH GRAYSON.

LAL Dinah Grayson's fresh, fewsome, an' free,
Wid a lilt iv her step an' a glent iv her e'e ;
She glowers ebbem at mé whativer I say,
An' meàstly mak's answer wid "M'appen I may!"
   "M'appen I may," she says, "m'appen I may ;
   Thou thinks I believe the', an' m'appen I may!"

Gay offen, when Dinah I manish to meet
O' Mūndays, i' t' market i' Cockerm'uth street,
I whisper, "Thou's nicer nor owte here to-day,"
An' she cocks up her chin an' says, "M'appen I may!
   M'appen I may, my lad, m'appen I may ;
   There's nowte here to crack on, an' m'appen I
     may!"

She's smart oot o' dooars—she's tidy i' t' hoose ;
Snod as a mowdy-warp—sleek as a moose.
I' blue goon, i' black goon, i' green goon or grey,
I tell her she's reeght, an' git "M'appen I may!"
   "M'appen I may," she'll say, "m'appen I may,
   Thou kens lal aboot, but m'appen I may!"

There's nūt mickle on her,—we ken 'at gud stuff
Laps up i' lal bundles, an' she's lal aneuf;
There's nowte aboot Dinah were better away
But her comical* ower-würd "M'appen I may."
   "M'appen I may," it's still, "m'appen I may."
   Whativer yan wants yan gits "m'appen I may!"

An' it shaps to be smittal; whoariver I gang,
I can't tell a stwory—I can't sing a sing—
I can't hod a crack, nay!—I can't read or pray
Widout bringin' in her dang't "M'appen I may."
   "M'appen I may," it cūms, "m'appen I may;"
   Asteed of Amen, I say "m'appen I may."

But she met me ya neeght aside Pards'aw Lea yatt—
I tock her seàf heàm, but I keep't her oot leàt,
An' offen I said i' my oan canny way,
"Will t'é like me a lal bit?"—Whey,—M'appen I
      may!
   M'appen I may, Harry—m'appen I may;
   Thou's rayder a hoaf-thick, but m'appen I may!"

I prist her to wed mé—I said I was pooar,
But eddlin aneuf to keep hung-er frayt' dooar.
She leuk't i' my feàce, an' than, hoaf turn't away,
She hung doon her heid an' said "M'appen I may!
   M'appen I may!"—(low doon)—"m'appen I may,
   I think thoo means fairly, an' m'appen I may."

   *Comical, used thus, means *Pert*, in central Cumberland.

Lal Dinah Grayson.

We're hingin' i't' bell reàps*—to t' parson I've toak't,
An' I gev him a hint as he maffelt an' jwoak't,
To mind when she sud say "love, honour, OBEY,"
'At she doesn't slip through wid her "M'appen I may."
   M'appen I may, may be—m'appen I may,
     But we moont put up than wid a "m'appen I may."

* During the period required for the publication of banns, a couple are said, figuratively, to be "hinging in t' bell ropes."

JWOHNNY, GIT OOT!

"Git oot wid the', Jwohnny, thou's no'but a fash;
Thou'll come till thou raises a desperat clash;*
Thou's here ivery day just to put yan aboot,
An' thou moiders yan terrably—Jwohnny, git oot!

What says t'e? I's bonnie? Whey! That's nowte
    'at's new.
Thou's wantin a sweetheart?—Thou's hed a gay few!
An' thou's cheatit them, yan efter t' t'udder, nèa
    doubt;
But I's nūt to be cheatit sèa—Jwohnny, git oot!

There's plenty o' lads i' beàth Lamplugh an' Dean
As yabble as thee, an' as weel to be seen;
An' I med tack my pick amang o' there aboot—
Does t'é think I'd ha'e thee, than? Hut, Jwohnny,
    git oot!

    * Clash—*Scandal.*

What? Nūt yan amang them 'at likes mé sa weel?
Whey, min—there's Dick Walker an' Jonathan Peel
Foorsettin' mé ola's i' t' lonnins aboot,
Beàth wantin' to sweetheart mé—Jwohnny, git oot!

What?—Thou will hev a kiss?—Ah, but tak't if
 thou dar!
I tell the', I'll squeel, if thou tries to cŭ' nār.
Tak' care o' my collar—Thou byspel, I'll shoot.
Nay, thou sha'n't hev anudder—Noo Jwohnny, git
 oot!

Git oot wid the', Jwohnny—Thou's tew't me reet sair;
Thou's brocken my comb, an' thou's toozelt my hair.
I willn't be kiss't, thou unmannerly loot!
Was t'ere iver sec impidence! Jwohnny, git oot!

Git oot wid the', Jwohnny—I tell the', be deùn.
Does t'e think I'll tak' up wid Ann Dixon's oald sheùn?
Thou ma' gā till Ann Dixon, an' pu' hur aboot,
But thou s'alln't pu' me, sèa—Jwohnny, git oot!

Well! That's sent him off, an' I's sworry it hes;
He med ken a lass niver means hoaf 'at she says.
He's a reet canny fellow, howiver I floot,
An' it's growin o' wark to say "Jwohnny, git oot!"

THE RUNAWAY WEDDING.

My fadder said "Nay"—an' my mudder said
 "Niver!"
When Willie furst telt them we wantit to wed;
We mud part—they said, beàth—part at yance an'
 for iver,
 An' she deavet me to deeth aboot foats 'at he hed.
A sailor was Will, forret, free-tonguet, an' funny,
 An' gi'en till o' manner o' teulment was he;
Rayder lowce i' religion, an' careless o' money,
 But dear was my wild thowtless Willie to me.

His life seemed meàd up of arrivin's an' sailin's—
 Rough hardship at sea, an' fair daftness at heàm.
I cry't ow'r his danger—I pray't ow'r his failin's,
 An' offen forgev what I cudn't but bleàm.
An' many a frind an' relation, an' neighbour
 Brong hints an' queer teàls aboot Will to poor me;
But neighbours an' frinds gat the'r pains for the'r
 labour,
 For t' màir they misco't him t' mair thowte on
 was he.

The Runaway Wedding. 37

An' t' upshot of o' the'r fine hints an' advices
   Was 'at, ya neet, weel happ't i' Will's greet sailor
      cwoat,
We dreàv, afoor dayleet, to Foster Penrice's,
   An' slip't ow'r till Annan i' t' Skinburneese bwoat.
An' theer we wer' weddit, i' their way o' weddin';—
   I dudn't hafe like't, but they said it wad dee;
An' I dār-say it may'd—for a lass 'at was bred in
   Their ways—but it wasn't like weddin' to me.

An' when Will brong me back, varra shām-feàcet
      an' freetent,
   Ower t' sin an' disgrace on't my mūdder went
      wild.—
Sair, sair dud my heart sink, but bravely it leeten't
   When Will prist me close up beside him, an' smil'd.
My fadder said lāl, no'but whishtit my mudder,
   An' pettit an' blest me wid tears iv his e'e;
Till beàth on us ru't what hed gi'en him sec bodder,
   An' shām't of our darrak steud Willie an' me.

Eigh—for loave, he was kind! an' he wad hev us
      weddit,
   As t' rest of his barnes hed been—menseful an'
      reet—
He leuk't at oor Scotch weddin'-writin' an' read it,
   But went up to t' Priest's aboot t' license that neet.

An' he keep't me at heàm, though we hed a hoose
    riddy.
He said he mud hev me, while Will follow't t' sea.
An' Will! weddin' meàd him douce, careful, an'
    stiddy,
An' he's hoddenly been a gud husband to me.

He seun hed a ship of his oan, an' meàd money,
    An' seàv't it, what he reckoned harder by far;
An', ola's weel-natur't, free-heartit an' funny,
    He meàd his-sel frinds wid whativer com' nār.
An' es for my mūdder, 'at thowte me so silly,
    An' lang nowte but bad i' poor Willie wad see,
I's thenkful she leevet to say—"Bless thee *son* Willie,
    "Many cūmforts we've hed, but meàst cūmfort i'
    thee."

BILLY WATSON' LONNING.

O for Billy Watson' lonnin' of a lownd summer neeght!
When t' stars come few an' flaytely, efter weerin'
    oot day-leeght—
When t' black-kite blossom shews itsel' i' hafe-seen
    gliffs o' grey,
An' t' honey-suckle's scentit mair nor iver it is i' t'
    day.
An' nūt a shadow, shap' or soond, or seeght, or
    sign 'at tells
'At owte 'at's wick comes santerin' theer but you,
    yer oan two sel's.
Ther' cannot be anudder spot so private an' so sweet,
As Billy Watson' lonnin' of a lownd summer neeght!

T' Hempgarth Broo's a cheersome pleàce when t'
    whins bloom full o' flooar—
Green Hecklebank turns greener when it's watter't
    wid a shooar—
There's bonnie neuks aboot Beckside, Stocks-hill,
    an' Greystone Green—
High Woker Broo gi'es sec a view as isn't offen seen—

It's glorious doon ont' Sandy-beds when t' sun's just
    gān to set—
An' t' Clay-Dubs isn't far aslew when t' wedder isn't
    wet;
But nin was meàd o' pūrpose theer a bonnie lass to
    meet
Like Billy Watson' lonnin' of a lownd summer neeght.

Yan likes to trail ow'r t' Sealand-fields an' watch for
    t' comin' tide,
Or slare whoar t' Green hes t' Ropery an' t' Shore
    of ayder side—
T' Weddriggs road's a lāl-used road, an' reeght for
    coortin toke—
An' Lowca' lonnin's reeght for them 'at like a
    langsome woke—
Yan's reeght aneuf up t' Lime-road, or t' Waggon-
    way, or t' Ghyll,
An' reeght for ram'lin's Cūnning-wood or Scatter-
    mascot hill.
Ther's many spots 'at's reeght aneuf, but nin o'
    ways so reeght
As Billy Watson' lonnin' of a lownd summer neeght.

Sec thowtes as thur com' thick lang sen to yan, a
    lonterin' lad,
Wid varra lal to brag on but a sperrit niver sad,

Billy Watson' Lonning.

When he went strowlin' far an' free aboot his sea-side
    heàm,
An' stamp't a mark upon his heart of ivery frind-like
    neàm ;—
A mark 'at seems as time drees on to deepen mair
    an' mair—
A mark 'at ola's breeghtens meàst i' t' gloom o'
    comin' care ;
But nowte upon his heart has left a mark 'at hods
    so breeght
As Billy Watson' lonnin' of a lownd summer neeght!

Oor young days may'd be wastet sair, but dār their
    mem'ry's dear !
And what wad yan not part wid noo ageàn to hev
    them here ?
Whativer trubles fash't us than, though nayder leet
    nor few,
They niver fash't us hafe so lang as less an's fash
    us noo ;
If want o' thowte brong bodderment, it pass't for
    want o' luck,
An' what cared we for Fortun's bats, hooiver feurce
    she struck ?
It mud be t' time o' life 'at meàd oor happiness
    complete
I' Billy Watson' lonnin' of a lownd summer neeght!

LONE AND WEARY.

Deid winter's nūt sa dark to me
    As t' lang leet days o' t' spring;—
I hate to see a swallow flee,
    Or hear a throssle sing;
I greàn 'at t' fresh green leaves on t' trees;
    I turn frae t' flooers o' May,
For t' croft was white wid dog-daisies
    When Jwohn was teàn away.

We coortit lang, dud Jwohn an' me—
    We waitit lang an' sair—
He thowte oor weddin' mūdn't be
    While beàth war poor an' bare;
An' sep'rat', I gat past my prime,
    Jwohn barrow-back't an' grey;
Reet sair I grudg't that wastit time,
    When Jwohn was teàn away.

Jwohn pinch't an' spar't, an' tew't an' streàv,
    Till t' heart wid-in him brak'—
Still aimin' brass aneuf to seàv,
    Some lal bit farm to tak':

Lone and Weary. 43

An' when he'd gitten t' farm an' me,
   'Twas plain he mūdn't stay ;—
He dwined through t' winter dark an' dree—
   I' t' spring was teàn away.

We máy'd hed many a happy year,
   If thowte to t' winds we'd flung,
An' join't oor strength life's leàd to beear,
   When beàth war lish an' yūng :
But widder't was oor flooer o' life
   Afoor oor weddin' day ;
An' I'd nūt been ya year a wife
   When Jwohn was teàn away.

Sooa t' spring o' life na sūmmer browte,
   To my poor man or me ;
An' t' spring o' t' year noo brings me nowte
   But t' mind o' misery.
I can't see what anudder sees
   I' t' fields an' t' flooers o' May,
For t' croft was white wid dog-daisies
   When Jwohn was teàn away.

T' CLEAN NED O' KES'ICK.

This phrase is proverbial in central Cumberland, and is generally used in a negative sense; thus, of a person whose character for upright conduct will not bear the full light of day, it is said, "He's nūt t' clean Ned o' Kes'ick."

Lang an' leàt we ma' lait throo fray Fiend's-fell*
    to Fles'ick,†
Afooar we'll finnd mair ner yā fellow or two
Yan can fairly an' freely co' t' clean Ned o' Kes'ick;
Oald Cūm'erlan' t'sel' on't hods no'but a few!
An' hoo mūn us tell when we div happen on them?
    Whey, that, just off-hand, isn't easy to say!
But sūm of o' yages hev marks plain upon them
    Showin' they're nin o' t' clean Ned o' Kes'ick—
        nūt they!

We ma' leet on a barne wid t' leùk of ill-natur'
    An' spite glowerin' oot of a widderful feàce;
A lean, discontentit, cross, gyversome creetur',
    'At kens hoo to mak' its-sel' t' maister o' t' pleàce—

---

* Fiend's-fell, an old name for Cross-fell, on the eastern verge of the county.

† The beautiful secluded bay which divides the two Heads of St. Bees, the most westerly points of Cumberland, is called Fleswick.

T' clean Ned o' Kes'ick.

'At yowls when it wants owte, an' glumps when it
    gits it,
Till o' but it's mūdder wad droon't iv a kit;
An' t' mair 'at she dantles, an' pampers, an' pets it,
    T' less like to growe t' clean Ned o' Kes'ick
        growes it.

Or mayhap, a lāl lad 'at tells teàls of his brudders,
    An' cocks his-sel' up, an example to t' rest—
'At seàvs his oan laikins an' laiks wid anudder's,
    An' geaps for owte gud like a gorb iv a nest;
'At boggles at lowpy-back, rack-ups, or shinny,
    An' keeps his-sel' ootside o' t' ruck at foot-bo';—
They ma' praise him 'at hes him—I'd lay my last
        guinea,
    He s' niver be t' clean Ned o' Kes'ick for o'.

Or a rovin' yūng chap 'at ga's hard efter t' lasses,
    An' stuffs them wid o' maks o' flaitchment an' lees;
Ol'a's smùrkin' an' smilin' an' fair to the'r feàces,
    But skiftin' his mattie as fancy ma' please—
Tackin' up at t' lang last, efter feùlin a duzzen,
    Wid sūmbody's dowter he thinks weel to dee;—
A taggelt like that sūd be hatit like puzzen—
    He'll niver be t' clean Ned o' Kes'ick, nūt he!

Or a man 'at likes brass, an' cheats o' maks o' ways
    for't,
  An' clowks at advantage whoariver he can;
An' taks drink gaily free when anudder chap pays
    for't,
  But wi'n't stand his share iv a shot like a man:
'At ol'a's for sūm dūrty profit ligs watchin';
  'At keeps o' he cares for anonder ya hat;
An' pays what he owes fwok wid phraisin' or
    fratchin'—
    He munnet be t' clean Ned o' Kes'ick—moon't
      that!

Or a swaddlin' oald sneak, wid a snowk an' a snivel,
  'At kests up his e'en when he hears a rūff jwoke;
Co'in sangs an' queer stwories o' 'ticements o' t'
    divel—
  An' snirrups his nwose up at t' praise o' poor fwok:
'At grùnts ageàn wrusslin's, fairs, hoond-trails an'
    reàces,
  An' sec-like divarsions, as sinful an' vain,
Winkin' hard at t' seàm time at wār sins i' hee
    pleàces—
    He niver was t' clean Ned o' Kes'ick—that's plain.

Nay! for be what it may be—his yeàge, steàt or
    station,
  A man hollow heartit, unfrindly, unfair,
Makin' mair nor reet use of a lofe or occasion,—
  Grippin' hard by his oan, an' still grankin' for mair;

'At can toak like a bishop, an' hod back his meanin',
  But can't wid his neighbours or kinsfwoke agree;
Keepin' bleàmin' an' backbitin', grudgin' an' pleenin'—
  He cannot be t' clean Ned o' Kes'ick—can't he.

BEN WELLS.

Kersmas is hardly Kersmas noo!—
    Nowte's left like what it used to be—
T' yall's nūt what they used to brew—
    An' t' fūn's nūt what we used to see—
T' lasses irn't hoaf sa smart,
    For o' the'r fallal hats an' veils,
An' music niver stūrs yan's heart
    Like "T' Hūnt's Up" played by oald Ben Wales.

"T' Hūnt's Up" of a Kersmas mworn,
    When stars war breet an' frost was keen,
Wad roose us like a hunter's whorn,
    Whativer hakes ower neet we'd seen.
An' dar! 'twas nice to snūg i' bed,
    An' lissen oot that brave oald lilt,
An' hear, at ivery stave they played,
    Gud wishes shootin' t' chorus till 't.

Ben Wales's fiddle, many a neet,
    Gev weel oiled springs to t' heaviest heels,
For few cud whyet hod the'r feet
    When Ben strack up his heartenin' reels.

Ben Wells.

Wid elbow room an' rozel't weel,
    Swinge! how he'd mak' fwoke keàv an' prance;
An' nowte cud match t' sly fiddle-squeal
    'At signall'd kiss i' t' cushion dance.

Noo, poor Ben Wales is deid an' geàn—
    His marrow willn't seùn be seen;
But rare top dancers many a yan,
    He's left to keep his memory green.
Nèa mair at ball or oald-fwoke's-neet
    We'll see his gud reet elbow jog;
An' when they laid Ben oot o' seet,
    T' oald cushion dance went oot o' vogue.

Fwoke's ways turn different, t' langer t' mair,
    An' what, lang sen, was reet 's grown wrang;
We're, meàst on us, owre fine to care
    For heàmly dance, teùn, teàl, or sang.
An' nowte's meàd varra lastin' here,
    T' best bow-hand growes oald an' fails,
·An' t' lishest legs git num' an' queer;
    Few last sa weel as oald Ben Wales.

NOTE.

The late Benjamin Wells was, for about half a century, the best known and most popular of all the dancing-masters who have plied their vocation amongst the country people of West Cumberland; and, as a teacher of the old-fashioned style of dancing, in which vigour, activity, and precision are, rather than gracefulness, the main *desiderata*, he has never been surpassed. As a violin player his performance was remarkably correct, distinct, and strongly marked as to time—in fact, the best possible fiddling to dance to. The last time I met with him was about twenty years ago, in the bar-parlour of an inn in the southern part of the Lake district, which was somewhat out of his ordinary beat, and where the strains of his fiddle, produced at my request, caused such excitement that a general and very uproarious dance (of males only) set in, and was kept up with such energy that, the space being confined, the furniture was seriously damaged, and Ben was at last ejected by the landlady as the readiest, indeed the only method of putting a stop to the riot. He was light, muscular, and springy, and, in his earlier years, wonderfully swift of foot, so much so that the late Dr. Johnstone, of Cockermouth, told me that he once (at Scale Hill) saw him, without any assistance, run down and capture a wild rabbit—a proof of activity rarely paralleled. Poor old Ben! It will be long ere his erect, compact little figure, his bright, cheery expression, his sprightly address, and his quick firm step are altogether forgotten in the western dales and seaward parishes of Cumberland. REQUIESCAT!

SANNTER, BELLA!

Sannter, Bella!—Bliss the', sannter,
    Th'u'll be seun aneuf at heàm;
Gā'n frae t' chūrch at sec a cannter,
    Fwoke 'll sweer th'u's thinkin' shām'—
Shām' 'at I sud woak aside the'!
    Does t'e, Bella, shām' o' me?
Whey than, bide the', dar it, bide the'!—
    Few's sa leet o' t' feut as thee.

See's t'e, Bella, nay but, see's t'e,
    Hoo th'u's makin' t' ne'bours laugh;
Th'u's a taistrel fair 'at is t'e,
    But I like thee weel——Hŭt, shaff!—
Whoa can tell his stwory rūnnin?—
    Whoa can coort an' win a reàce?—
If th'u's flay't I's foase, or fūnnin',
    Stop, an' leuk me fair i' t' feàce!

Leuk, an' see if I wad cheat the'—
    Leuk, I tell the', glimes wont dee!
Whativer wrang't the', I wad reet the',
    Whoa-iver fails the', trust i' me.

Wait! Nay, tak' mair time, I pray the'—
  Shūttin' frae yan like a dart—
Nowte for nowte I's axin' frae the'—
  Nowte for nowte, but heart for heart.

Sannter, than! Nay, Bella, sannter!
  I'll nūt say ya wūrd 'at's wrang,
But th'u's a wannter!—I's a wannter!
  An' nowder sud be wannters lang.
Thoo kens what sec a heàm I've gitten—
  Kens o' 's reet, an' straight, an' square—
Kens o' wad fit the' like a mitten;
  What the hangment wad t'e mair?

Sannter! sannter!! sannter, Bella!!!
  Gi' me time to tell my teàl;
'Tis n't kind to mak' a fellow
  T' laughin-stock of hoaf o' t' deàl.
Does t'e think o' 's nūt fairation?
  Hes t'e any foat to finnd?
Nay! Whey than, ther's nèa 'casion—
  Hŭh—By jing, I's oot o' wind!

'Beàt thy speed! Dar sonn, I'll ho'd the'!
  Ho'd the' till I've said my say—
Till my heart's ya wish I've shew'd the',
  Gittin' back for 't ey or nay.

Sannter, Bella!

Wil't'e than, say, wil't'e wed me?
  Ah! Thou wadn't still say—no!
Faith! a bonnie dance th'u's led me,
  But that lāl squeeze mak's up for o'!—

T' squeeze frae thy smo' fing-ers, Bella!
  Trimlin' here i' my rough hand;
It's queer a touch sa leet can tell a
  Teàl sa plain to understand;
It's queerer thoo sūd be sa freeten't,—
  Flay't when nowte at o' 's amiss.
Loavin'! How thy feàce hes breeten't,
  Reedenin' ūp at t' furst fair kiss.

BRANTHET NEUK BOGGLE.

(A TEAL FOR A WINTER NEEGHT.)

'At Marron Beck's a bonnie beck, what mazelin wad deny?
An' what compares wi' Branthet Neùk 'at Marron Beck gā's by?
Wid hooses white, an' worchets green, an' Marron runnin' clear,
Eigh! Branthet Neùk's a heartsome spot i' t' sūnny time o' year!

But loave! it is a dowly pleàce when winter neeghts growe lang;
For t' lwoan ligs dark atween its banks,—a flaysome rwoad to gang
When t' wind rwoars wild in t' trees abeùn, an' Marron rwoars below,—
An' Branthet Neuk's a hantit spot, as I've some reeght to know.

They say a heidless woman woaks at sartin neeghts
    o' t' year,
An' greàns an' yewls at sec a rate as freeghtens
    fwoke to hear ;
I wadn't mind sec teàls, but yance I gat a freeght
    me-sel'
I' Branthet Neùk, an' hoo it was, just lissen an' I'll
    tell.

Yā neeght, lang sen, at Cursmass time, wid
    Cursmass mak' o' wedder,
A lock on us at Branthet met, to hev a glass togidder;
We crack't, an' jwok't, an' drank, an' smeuk't, while
    hoaf o' t' neeght went by,
For Isbel Simon' drink was gud, an' we war rayder
    dry!

'Twas lownd an' leàt—past yan o'clock—wid nūt a
    spark o' moon :
An' like a clood o' cardit woo', thick snow keep't
    sinkin' doon,
When reeght up t' Neùk three Jwohn's an' me went
    wādin' heàm through t' snow—
Jwohn Suntan, an' Jwohn Bell o' t' Rayes, an'
    Jwohn o' Craypless Ho'.

We'd gitten hoaf o' t' way up t' lwoan,—nār Edard
    Beeby' yat,
An' theear we stopp't, for marcy me! a parlish
    freeght we gat,
Lood greàns we heard—lang hollow beels, 'at shak't
    oor varra beàns,
"For God-seàk, lads, mak on," sez yan, "them's t'
    heidless woman' greàns!"

"But nay," sez I, "if wantin' t' heid, she raises sec
    a rout,
I'd like to see what way she taks to fetch sec
    haybays oot;
They say yan stops a woman's noise when yan taks
    off her heid,
But this, by gock! wad mak yan sweer they're noisy
    whick or deid."

It's Burns 'at sez Jwohn Barleycworn can mak yan
    bold as brass;
An' Isbel' drink meàd me quite keen this greànin'
    thing to feàce.
We shootit Edard Beeby up an' meàd 'im git a
    leeght—
He grummel't sair to be disturb't at sec a time o'
    neeght,

But brong yan oot;—an', led bee t' lugs, we follow't
    efter t' soond,
While clwose t' swine-hull dooar we com, an' stopt,
    an' gedder't roond.
"By gockers, lads!" Jwohn Suntan said, "It's no'but
    Edard' swine!"
"Nay, nay," sez Edard, "mine's i' soat—it's nèa
    pig o' mine!"

"Well, I'll gā in, an' see," sez I. O' t' rest steud
    leukin on
As in I creept wid t' leeght, an' fund greit lang Joe
    Nicholson
Hoaf cover't up wid mucky strea,—soond asleep,—
    and *snworin'*,
As if o' t' bulls o' Dean war theear, an' ivery bull
    was rwoarin'.

We trail't him oot, an' prop't him up ageàn t' oald
    swine-hull wo'—
An' dazet wid coald he glower't aboot, an' dadder't
    like to fo'—
We help't 'im in, an' hap't 'im weel, on t' squab
    aback o' t' dooar,
He said his wife had barr't 'im oot, as oft she'd
    deun afooar.

Sez Jwohn o' t' Rayes, "If iv'ry neeght he maks sa
  gurt a din,
It's rayder queer a wife like his sud iver let 'im in;
It's varra weel we hārd 'im though, he med ha'
  dee't o' coald!
Come, let's git heàm!"—an' laughin' loud, we lonter't
  oot o' t' foald.

Jwohn Suntan's rwoad left oor's gay seun, an' sooa
  dud Jwohn Bell's,
An' Jwohn o' Craypless Ho' an' me went poapin on
  oorsells,
An' no'but slow, for t' snow was thick, an' meàd it
  bad to woke,
Sooa mid-leg deep we striddel't on, but offen steud
  to toke.

Jwohn hed a faymish crack in 'im,—his fadder hed
  afooar 'im,—
At teàls àn' sangs, an' sec like fun not many cud cum
  ower 'im;
An' theàr an' than, dud Jwohn set on, at t' furst gud
  rist we teuk,
To tell me hoo ther com to be a ghost i' Branthet
  Neùk.

Branthet Neuk Boggle.   59

Sez Jwohn, sez he, "I' Branthet Neùk, as varra weel
    thoo knows,
'Tween t' beck an' Edard Beeby' hoose ther stands
    some brocken wo's;
Lang sen, when they hed roofs on them, yance,
    leàtish on i' t' year,
Some tinkler fwoke gat leave fray t' lword, an' com
    to winter theear.

"Two oald fwoke, wid a scrowe o' barns, an' yā
    son, jūst a man,—
A handy chap to shap' a speun, or cloot a pot or
    pan,—
An' this chap hed a bonnie wife, 'at dūdn't leuk like
    t' rest,
But fair, clean-skinn't, an' leàdy-like, an' ol'as nicely
    drest.

"An' hoo she com to be wid them was niver reeghtly
    known,
But nebbers so' she wasn't used as if she'd been ther
    oan;
For t' oald fwoke soas't her neet an' day,—her man
    —a dūrty tike!—
Wad bray her wid a besom-stick, a thyvel, or sec
    like;

"Tull yance a nebber teùk her in, when t' tinklers
    flang her oot,
An' she let fo' a würd or two 'at brong a change
    aboot;
She telt o' sūm stown geese an' sheep, an' whoar
    they hed them hidden;
Of mutton up on t' sleeping loft, an' skins anonder
    t' midden.

"It wasn't many würds she said,—but würds she
    said anew
To bring t' oald tinkler and her man tull what was
    weel ther due;
For lang i' Cārel jail they laid, an' when t' assize
    com on,
T' Jūdge let t' oald waistrel lowce ageàn, but hang't
    his whopeful son.

"An' back frae Cārel t' tinkler com, to Branthet
    reeght away,
An' 'ticet t' poor lass frae t' nebber's hoose whoar
    she'd been fain to stay;
He promish't fair to treat her weel, an' dūd while t'
    seckint neeght,
An' than, (reeght pleas't was Branthet fwok,) he
    meàd a moonleeght fleeght.

Branthet Neuk Boggle. 61

"An' days went by an' neàbody went nār to t'
    tinkler's dooar,
At last some barns peep't in an' so' some huller't
    bleùd on t' flooar,
An' than t' hoose dooar was drūven in, an' sec a
    seeght was theer,
'At sūm 'at so' 't went reid wid reàge, an' sūm went
    white wid fear.

"Squeez't up intull a dūrty neùk, an' bleùdy, stark,
    an' deid,
They fūnd that nice young lass's corp, bit niver
    fūnd her heid ;
T' oald tinkler hoond hed hagg't it off afooar he
    meàd a fleeght on 't,
An' teàn it wid him, fwoke suppwos't, to gud his-sel'
    wid t' seet on't.

"An' nin o' t' clan at efter that i' t' country side was
    seen.
But iver sen a hantit spot hes that Neùk-lonning
    been,
For t' mūrder't woman wokes aboot, an' greàns, for
    o' she's deid,
As lood as what we hārd to-neeght,—*they say she
    laits her heid!*"

"Wey, weel deùn, Jwohn!" to Jwohn sez I, "an'
    thenks ta for thy teàl,
It's meàd me hoaf forgit hoo t' snow maks o' my
    teeàs geàl;
Th'u's just at heàm,—gud neeght, my lad, but fūrst
    hear this fray me,
If iv'ry teàl 'at's telt be true, thy stwory's neà lee!"

MARY RAY AN' ME.

Bonnie Mary Ray an' me
   Wer' barnish sweethearts lang,
But I was wild an' yūng, an' she
   Was niver reetly strang;
Sooa frinds o' beàth sides threep't it sair
   'At partit we sud be—
An' life was darken't t' lang-er t' mair
   To Mary Ray an' me.

But yance lāl Mary Ray an' me
   Met oot on Woker Broo,
When t' clouds burn't reid far oot at sea,
   An' t' sūn com' bleezin' through,
An' sent ya lang-droan glissenin' gleam
   Across that dowly sea,
Like t' leetenin' up o' life's dark dream
   To Mary Ray an' me.

An' "Sees t'e, Mary Ray," I says,
   "That lang low line o' leet;—
It cūms to say oor leàter days
   May yit be fair an' breet,

An' t' cloods 'at darken owre us noo
    May rive like yon we see,
An' t' sūn o' love cūm glentin through,
    To shine on thee an' me."

But Mary lean't her sinkin heid
    Ageàn my heavin' breist.
"Tūrn roond," she said, "an' say asteed,
    What reads t'e here i' t' East;
For t' East's mair sure to guide us reet,
    If dark an' coald it be;
It's liker life—nor that reid leet—
    To Mary Ray an' thee."

I turn't an' leùk't wid bodeful glooar,
    Whoar o' was coald an' gray,
An' like a ghost reàse t' white church tooar,
    To freeten whope away;
An' Woker's shadow heap't a gloom
    Owre beck, an' field, an' tree,
'At said far darker days mud cūm
    To Mary Ray an' me.

An' niver mair on' Woker Broo
    I strowl't wid Mary Ray;
They partit us that winter through—
    An' than I went away.

An' Mary in t' churchyard they'd laid
  When I com' back frae t' sea ;
'Twas true what Woker's shadow said
  To Mary Ray an' me.

THE BANNASYDE "CAIRNS."

(IN THE DIALECT OF HIGH FURNESS.)

T' yer jornas ooer Wa'na Scar to Seeathet ye'll offen aneeuf ha nooatis't a lot o' round heeaps o' steeans strinklet heear an' theear ooer t' feeace o' Bannasyde mooer: an' if ye leuk inta them fine maps 'at t' güverment's putten owt ye'll see 'at t' pleeace 'at's meeant for Bannasyde hes *cairns, cairns, cairns* dottit o' ooer 't. They wor sharp fellows wor t' surveyors 'at went ooer t' grund ùt meeak thor maps. Yā lot o' them com' efter anudder for iver sa many years, sūm wi' red cooats an' sūm wi'out; an' they teeuk for iver o' pains wi' the'r wark. Why, when yee yersel' gat a lile lūmp off āld Geoordie Flimming' field ùt meeak yer bit of a gardin, efter they'd survey't an' mizzer't it, they went o' ooer t' grūnd a-fresh, just ùt put it in; an' theear it is i' t' maps, as plain as t' field its-sel'.

The Bannasyde Cairns. 67

Bit about thor cairns. I mun tell yé 'at when I furst hard o' them, I cùdn't meeak end nor side o' what they cud be, an' I went tull Rodger Forness ut ex about them. Rodger kna's meear about sike things nor a deeal o' fooak; sooa I went tull him, an' he telt mé 'at cairns was heeaps o' lilely steeans 'at hed been rais't ooer t' graves o' girt men lang sen, afooer ther was any kirk-garths ut bury t'em in —'at Dunmal Raise is t' biggest cairn i' t' country, an' 'at it was pilet up ooer a king 'at was kil't theear. Rodger an' me hed a gūd laugh togidder ooer t' Bannasyde cairns, for we beeath kna't gaily weel how *they* com to be theear, but we said t' yan til't' tudder, "Let's hear, an' see, an' say nowte."

Bit howiver, when them 'cute ordnance chaps, as they co't thersel's, was teean in wi' thor heeaps, it's lile wūnder 'at a gentleman 'at leev't here—yan Mr. Rowlins, sud ha' meead his-sel' cock suer 'at they wor nowder meear nor less nor sooa many lile Dunmal Raises, an' thowte he wod like ut see what they hed in belā' t'em; an' as it wodn't be like a gentleman ut keep o' t' fun till his-sel', he ex't a lot of udder gentlemen, frinds o' his, mainly what parsons, fray aboot Ooston, ut come an' see t' cairns oppen't, an' t' grūnd under t'em groven up, ut finnd out what they cūver't.

Well! they o' torn't up true to t' day. Ald Billy Bamthet, Tommy Thackra, an' yan or two meear Cunniston chaps hed been hired ut due t' wark, an' away they o' went, out on Bannasyde, an' at it they set.

O' t' fun 'at they gat, howiver, was a bit of laugh noos an' thans at āld Bamthet. He was a queer āld dog was Bamthet, an' he keep't exin' on them o' manner o' questions about what they wor laitin on. At ya time he wod say till a parson varra seriously, " Irr yé expectin' ut̩ finnd a Bishop ? " at anudder he wod ex t'em if they thowte Moses was buriet theear. Bit nowte's nowte, whativer may be laitit for ! an' suer aneuf ther' was nowte ut be fūnd under t' heeaps o' steeans.

It was a cāld, sleety, slattery sooart of a day o' through, but they steeak tull the'r wark like Britons, tull it was turnin' sooa dark 'at āld Bamthet says, " Irr we ut hod at it any lang-er, Mr. Rowlins ? Tommy Thackra's gittin' terrable teer't, an' it's growan sooa dark 'at we'll seeùn nit be yable ut say whedder what we may finnd be t' beeans of a bishop or t' beeans of a billy-gooat, wi'out ther's some amang ye 'at knā's beeans by greeapin' at 'em."

Well, they o' thowte they mud give it up for a bad job. They'd torn't ooer meear nor a scooer o' t' steean heeaps, an' they hedn't fūnd sa mich as t' shin beean of a cracket ut egg 'em on any farder. Sooa Mr. Rowlins tel't his men ut gidder up the'r hacks an' the'r speeads an' things, an' git away heeam.

As they wor o' trailin away varra slā' an' varra

whishtly, down Willy Garnett girt intak', āld Bamthet sidelt up till amang t' gentlemen, an' says, "Now, Mr. Rowlins," says he, "just tell us what ye thowte was to be fūnd i' t' clearin's o' t' Bracken-beds." "What do you call clearin's of Bracken-beds, William?" Mr. Rowlins ex't. "Why! dunnot yè knā," says Bamthet, "dunnot yè knā 'at t' farmers mā's t' brackens i' t' back-end, ut bed the'r beeas's wi'?" "Of course I know that," says Mr. Rowlins, "but what has mowing brackens to do with these cairns?" "Due wi' them?" says t' tudder, "why, ivery thing ut due wi' them! How d'yè think the'r leys wad cūm on if t' cobble steeans wor left liggin howe-strowe amang t' brackens when they com ut mā' t'em? They gidder 'em off, to be suer, an' pile 'em up into t' heeaps 'at we've been wrowkin' amang o' t' day, an' yee co' cairns. I rackon cairns is t' genteel wūrd for t' clearin's o' t' bracken-beds, bit I niver heer't 'em co't cairns afooer, an' I'll niver co' t'em cairns ageean—t' āld neeam's reet aneeuf for fellows like me!"

Well, when they heer't t'is, t' parsons leuk't at t' gentlemen, an' t' gentlemen leeuk't at t' parsons, an' than they leeuk't yan at t' tudder o' round as they steeud, an' than they brast out wi' a laugh loud aneeuf ut raise o' t' ravens on t' Bell Crag an' o' t' gleads i' Buckbarrow. Efter they'd whyeten't down a bit, Mr. Rowlins says, "Well but, William, why didn't you tell us this before?" "Nay, nay," says t' āld thief, "I wosn't gā'n ut spoil yer day's spooart i' that fashi'n, when ye'd browte yer frinds sa far ut see't. That wodn't ha' been manners!" An' away down t' intak' he went sneeakin an' sniggerin till Tommy Thackra an' t' rist o' them. But Tommy an' t' rist o' them didn't snigger back ageean. They o' growl't at him, an' yan o' them said, "It's an āld tūrkey! What for cudn't it hod t' āld tūng on't till we'd gitten anudder gud day's weeage or two, an' plenty ut itt an' drink wi't, out o' t' clearin's o' t' bracken-beds? T'er's anew o' t'em left too ha' keep't us gā'n for a week!"

BETTY YEWDALE.

(Extract from a Lecture on "The People of the English Lake Country, in their Humorous Aspect."

STILL harping upon married life, I wish to draw your attention to one of the finest passages in Wordsworth's greatest poem— *The Excursion,* which abounds in fine passages. In that I refer to, the poet gives a very charming account of the daily life of a humble couple in Little Langdale, on whose hospitality he describes himself, or his hero, as being thrown, when benighted and lost in that narrow vale, where, as *I* have found occasionally, the closely encircling belt of high mountains makes a dark night very black indeed. The poet says—

> "Dark on my road the autumnal evening fell,
> And night succeeded with unusual gloom,
> So that my feet and hands at length became
> Guides better than mine eyes—until a light
> High in the gloom appeared, too high, methought,
> For human habitation."

Climbing the heights, however, he finds that the light proceeds from a lantern, held out by a woman to guide her husband homewards from the distant slate quarry. The poet proceeds to tell of his hospitable reception, the husband's arrival, and the unusual beauty of the goodman's face, adding—

> "From a fount
> Lost, thought I, in the obscurities of time,
> But honoured once, those features and that mien
> May have descended, though I see them here.
> In such a man, so gentle and subdued,
> Withal so graceful in his gentleness,
> A race illustrious for heroic deeds,
> Humbled, but not degraded, may expire."

Thus much for Jonathan Yewdale. His wife, Betty, is made to speak for herself—but to speak in language very different from that she really used, as may be seen in a still more remarkable work than that I quote from—*The Doctor*, namely, by Robert Southey, wherein Betty Yewdale, in her "oan mak' o' toke," relates "The true story of the terrible knitters of Dent." In *The Excursion*, however, she is made to speak thus—

> "'Three dark mid-winter months
> Pass,' said the Matron, 'and I never see,
> Save when the sabbath brings its kind release,
> My helpmate's face by light of day. He quits
> His door in darkness, nor till dusk returns.
> And through Heaven's blessing, thus we gain the bread
> For which we pray; and for the wants provide
> Of sickness, accident, and helpless age.

Betty Yewdale.

Companions have I many ; many friends,
Dependants, comforters—my wheel, my fire,
All day the house-clock ticking in mine ear,
The cackling hen, the tender chicken brood,
And the wild birds that gather round my porch.
This honest sheep-dog's countenance I read ;
With him can talk ; nor seldom waste a word
On creatures less intelligent and shrewd.
And if the blustering wind that drives the clouds
Care not for me, he lingers round my door,
And makes me pastime when our tempers suit ;—
But, above all, my thoughts are my support.'"

This no doubt is, as I have said, a very charming picture of humble house life in a lonely home; but the picture is drawn by a poet, and, in *his* words—certainly not in those of the worthy dame from whose lips they are made thus melodiously to flow.

I have conversed with many elderly people who knew this couple familiarly, and several have told me of the almost seraphic beauty of the old man's features, diluted, as it was, by a lack of expression, denoting a weakness of mind and character, which, in the opinion of neighbours, perfectly justified Betty in maintaining full domestic supremacy and undisputed rule.

Of the manner in which she sometimes asserted that supremacy, and brought her husband back to his allegiance, when, as was rare, he happened to stray from it, an amusing instance was told to me by a respectable widow, who for many years occupied the farm of Oxenfell, a lonely spot, amid the wild craggy uplands on the Lancashire side of Little Langdale, and nearly opposite to Hackett, where the Yewdales resided. Were it only to show how differently great poets and ordinary people regard the same subject, this is worthy of preservation, and I give it, very nearly, in my informant's own phraseology.

"Ther' hed been a funeral fray aboot t' Ho'garth, an' varry nār o' t' men fooak about hed geean wi' 't till Cūnniston. Nixt fooarneeun, Betty Yewdale com' through fray Hackett, an' says she till me, 'Hes yower meeaster gitten back fray t' funeral?' 'Nay,' says I, 'he hesn't!' 'An' irrn't ye gān ut lait him!' says Betty. 'Lait him!' says I, 'I wodn't lait him if he didn't cù heeam for a week.' 'Why, why!' says she, 'yee ma' due as ye like, but I mun bring mine heeam, an' I *will!*' An' off she set i' t' rooad till Cūnniston. On i' t' efterneeun, she co' back, driving Jonathan afooer her wi' a lang hezle stick—an' he sartly was a sairy object. His Sūnda' cleeas leeūk't as if he'd been sleepin i' them on t' top of a durty fluer. T' tye of his neckcloth hed wūrk't round till belā t' ya lug, an' t' lang ends on't hung ooer ahint his shou'der. His hat hed gitten bulged in at t' side, an' t' flipe on 't was cock't up beeath back an' frūnt. O' togidder, it wod ha' been a queerly woman body 'at wod ha' teean a fancy till Jonathan that day.

"Says I till Betty, 'What, ye *hev* fūnd him than?'

'Fūnd him!' says she, 'ey, I' fūnd him! I knā't whār ut lait him! I fūnd him at t' Black Bull, wi' yower meeaster, an' a lock meear o' t' seeam sooart. They wor just gān ut git the'r dinner, wi' a girt pan o' beef-steeaks set on t' middle o' t' teeable. I meead t' frying pan an' t' beef-steeaks flee gaily murrily oot o' t' duer, an' I set on an' geh them o' sike a blackin' as they willn't seeun forgit. Than I hail't Jonathan oot fray amang them; bit when I'd gitten him out wi' mè, I shām't ut be seen on t' rooads wi' him. Dud iver yè see sike a pictur'?' 'Why, nay! nit sa offen, indeed,' says I. 'Well,' says Betty, 'as I wodn't be seen i' t' rooads wi' him, we hed to teeak t' fields for't, an', as it wosn't seeaf ut let him climm t' wo's, I meead him creep t' hog-hooals.* I meead him creep t' hog-hooals,' says Betty, 'an' when I gat him wi' his heead in an' his legs out, I dūd switch him.'"

This true story shows Wordsworth's humble heroine in not quite so romantic a light as he throws round her in the passages I have quoted; but I don't see that it need lower her in our esteem.

---

* Hog-holes are small apertures left in the dry stone fences, to allow the sheep, oɪ *hogs*, to get through from one pasture to another.

THE SKULLS OF CALGARTH.

A Reminiscence of Windermere.

(CHIEFLY IN THE DIALECT OF WESTMORLAND.)

GREEN verged, glancing Wynander, first, fairest of our meres,
　How potent was the fairy charm, how perfect was the spell
That bound me to its beauty once in youth's untrammell'd years
And held me lingering, lingering at its Ferry's famed Hotel.

'Twas ere the railway whistle 'woke the echoes of the hills,
And Arnold the vivacious perch'd as yet behind the mail,

The Skulls of Calgarth. 77

And that fine old English autocratic Boniface, Ben
    Bills,*
Ruled with a wholesome despotism the Ferry and
    Hotel.

And Benjamin's chief ferryman was stalwart old
    John Long,
A veteran of the wrestling ring (its records hold his
    name,)
Who yet in life's late autumn was a wiry wight and
    strong,
Though grizzly were his elf-locks wild and bow'd his
    giant frame.

Cool Michaelmas its summer brought, serene, and
    soft, and gray;
The high steep wood of Harrowslack all yellow
    grew and sere,
And shower'd its faded raiment o'er the Ferry's
    gloom-girt bay—
The deepest, darkest, dreamiest nook of bay-fringed
    Windermere.

* Arnold and Bills, landlords of the Ferry at different periods—the first named having been previously the well known guard of the coach that traversed the Lake district.

And listlessly and idly as the lazy mists that rest,
Or cling with loving closeness, after summer's heats are gone,
And autumn's breezes over, to Wynander's placid breast—
The latest guest the Ferry held, I loitered there alone.

And there upon its calm-still'd wave, throughout the shortening day,
And oft when daylight waned apace, and stars be-gemm'd the sky,
By rocky nab or islet green, by slumb'ring pool or bay,
We glided through the peacefulness—stark old John Long and I.

Yes; though John Long was worn and wan, he still was stark and strong,
And he plied his bending "rooers" with a boatman's manly pride,
As crashing past the islands, through the reed stalks crisp and long,
He stretch'd away far northward, where the lake spread fair and wide.

"Now rest upon your oars, John Long," one
    evening still said I,
When shadows deepened o'er the mere from Latter-
    barrow Fell ;
For far beyond broad Weatherlam the sun sank in
    the sky,
And bright his levell'd radiance lit the heights
    around Hillbell.

"And tell me an old story," thus I further spoke,
    " John Long,
Some mournful tale or legend, of the far departed
    time ;
The scene is all too solemn here for lightsome lay
    or song,
So tell, and, in your plain strong words, I'll weave
    it into rhyme."

Then old John Long revolved his quid, and gaunt
    he look'd and grim—
For darker still athwart the lake spread Latter-
    barrow's shade—
And pointing o'er the waters broad to fields and
    woodlands dim,
He soberly and slowly spake, and this was what he
    said.

"A house ligs lā' an' leånsome theear, doon in that
 . oomer dark,
Wi' wide, heigh-risin' chimla-heeads, lā' roof, an'
   crum'lin' wo',
O' wedder-gnā'n an' weed-be-grown—for time hes
   setten t' mark
O' scooers an' scooers o' weearin' years on hantit
   Co'garth Ho'.

"T' āld Philipsons o' Windermer' lang, lang hed
 .   theer the'r heeam;⁽¹⁾
An' far an' wide the'r manors spread ooer forest,
   field, an' fell;
But now ther's nit i' t' cūntryside a steeatsman o'
   their neeam—
Ther's Philipsons, but o' work hard for breead like
   me mysel'.

"For niver thinkin' they'd aneeuf, and strivin' still
   for meear,
They wantit ivery scrap o' land the'r nebbers held
   aboot;
An' many a pooer man's grund they gat, by meeans
   nit ol'a's fair—
An' lang o' that grund-greed o' theirs, this teeal o'
   mine fell out.

The Skulls of Calgarth. 81

"An āld-ly man nār Burthet leev't, his neeam was
    Kraster Cook,
An' whyetly his life hed ron wi' Dorot'y his deeam.
A conny lile bit farm was theirs, a lown an' sunny
    neeuk,
An' t' hoose 'at's theear upon it still keeps up āld
    Kraster' neeam.

" Myles Philipson wad offen toak wi' Kraster Cook
    an' t' wife,
An' priss them hard the'r bit o' land ut swap wi'
    him or sell;
But beeath o' t'em at last spak' oot—they'd rayder
    part wi' life
Ner sell or swap a single yird of infield land or fell.

"'Ye s' part wi' 't than,' said Philipson, as rantin
    mad he rooar'd,
'I'll hev that bit o' land o' yours, sud yee be 'live
    or deead.'
An' Kraster fūnd 'at efter that as if ther was a sooard
'At hed to fo' when t' time co' round, still hingin'
    ooer his heead.

"Bit nowte com on't till t' Kersmas time, an' than
    till āld Co'garth
They went wi' t' tudder nebbors, kindly ex't to t'
    Kersmas feeast;
An' t' best o' t' seeats at t' sūpper booard, an'
    warmest neeuk at t' hearth
Wer' theirs, for t' squire hed ooerder't 'at they sud
    be that mitch greàc't.

"Bit seeun they fūnd that Kersmas treeat mud cost
    'em parlish dear,
For Philipson pertendit 'at they'd stown a silver cūp,
An' Cook's house was ratch't through an' through,
    an' t' silver cup fund theear,
Heead theear, girt like, o' purpose—an' t' āld cūpple
    wer' teean up.

"An' for the'r lives they triet 'em beeath, an' beeath
    condemn't to dee.
Myles Philipson was theear, an' Dolly glooer't him
    hard i' t' feeace,
As meear ner plowmb she rais't hersel', an', terrable
    ut see,
She spak' thir wūrds i' seccan a skrike as rung
    through t' justice pleeace :—

The Skulls of Calgarth.   83

"'Ey, gūd thysel', Myles Philipson—thou thinks
    th'u's mannish't grand ;
Thou thinks th'u's hooal't our lile bit grund, and
    gitten't o' for nowte,
Bit, harks t'e here, Myles Philipson—that teenie
    lump o' land
Is t' dearest grūnd a Philipson hès ayder stown or
    bowte ;

"'For yee sall prosper niver meear, yersel', nor yan
    o' t' breed ;
Whativer schemes yee set a geeat 'ill widder i' yer
    hand,
Whativer side yee tak' 'ill lwose ; an', spite of o' yer
    greed,
A time 'ill come when t' Philipsons wi' n't awn an
    inch o' land.

"An', while Co'garth's strang wo's sall stand, we'll
    hā'nt it neet an' day,
Ye s' niver mair git shot on us, whativer way yè tak' ;
Whativer plan or geeat yè try, ut banish us away,
Ye'll hardly knā' we irr away afooer ye see us back.

"An' suer aneeuf, neist Kersmas, when they'd nit
 been twelvemonth deead,
(They'd buriet t' pooer āld fooak wi' lime, whār the'
 wor putten doon,)
Two skulls steead in a hooel i' t' wo', aside o' t'
 wide stair heead,
At āld Co'garth, an' theear they gurn't, a warnin'
 fray aboon.

"An', ivery mak' o' pains they teeuk ut git 'em
 druven away—
They buriet them, they born't them weel, they
 bray't them till they brak',
They sunk 'em full't wi' leed i' t' lake, they pash't
 'em deep i' clay,
But just as Dolly said they wod, they still co' gurnin'
 back.

"An' theear they've gurn't an' gurn't ageean, for
 many a hundert year,
An' scooars o' fooak ha' seen 'em theear—it's neea
 lees I tell—
Till t' Bishop[2] wo't 'em up i' t' hooal, bit still
 they're gurnin' theear,
For just afooar he wo't 'em up, I seed them theear
 mysel'.

The Skulls of Calgarth.

"An' t' Philipsons went doon an' doon, the'r schemin' o' went wrang,
Though offen for a sinkin' coase they meead a gallant stand ;
Fray t' steeat rowls about Windermer' the'r neeam hes vanish't lang,
I divn't knā' a Philipson 'at hods an inch o' land."

NOTES.

1. In a foot-note to *West's Guide to the Lakes*, published first about 1770—its 5th edition being dated 1793—the author or editor suggests certain other modes of accounting for the presence of the famous skulls of Calgarth, but fails in offering anything so satisfactory as the popular version here done into rhyme. The writer of the note appears to have seen them himself, and I have known more than one old person, besides John Long, who averred that in their youth, they had seen the said remains occupying their immemorial position. The misfortunes of the Philipsons of Calgarth and Crook are matter of local history, and with some of their recorded exploits, make them, perhaps, the most interesting family of the two counties.

2. Dr. Watson, the celebrated Bishop of Llandaff, who acquired the estate of Calgarth, and long resided upon it, but not at the old Hall. He is always spoken of by the old people who remember him as " *T'* Bishop."

MAP'MENT.

(IN THE DIALECT OF HIGH FURNESS.)

Māp'ment—Martha—māp'ment!
  Thow knā'sn't what thow says—
An' thow fair torments my heart owt
  Wi' thy lile contrairy ways—
It's oa' a heeap o' māp'ment
  Ut say 'at this or that
Sūd meeak us put it off ageean—
  Thow toaks thow knā'sn't what!

We irrn't rich, an' mayn't be;
  What than!—wi' time an' keear,
An' pu'in' weel togidder,
  We may meeak our little meear.
We s' niver, I's insuer us,
  Be neeàk't or clemm'd or càld,
But spār' a ho'penny or two
  Ut cheer us when we're āld.

Map'ment.

Let's feeace it, Martha, feeace it,
    Whativer cūms behint!
God niver sends a mowth wi'owt
    A sūm'at ut put in't.
We s', happen, hev a mowth or two
    Ut feed besides owr ā'n,
What matter—they s' be welcome o'
    Ut share whativer's gā'n!

We s' ol'a's hing togidder weel,
    An' beeath du what we can—
A borden 's leeter shared by two,
    Nor when it's borne by yan.
But if we's plagued wi' trūbble,
    (An' whā's fray trūbble free?)
I' s' try ut lig thy share tull mine,
    An' kep it oa' fray thee.

An' if we's pooer, we s' sham' nin,
    For rich fooak's no'but fooak;
An' whā can tell, we s' happen drā
    Sūm' prize fray fortun's pooak.
But wrowte-for punds gā's farder far
    Nor hundreds 's gi'en or fūnd;
An' sūm' may be to t' fooer for t' barnes
    When we gā ūnder t' grūnd.

Map'ment.

Cūm let's hev neā meear māp'ment,
    But gradely feeace owr chance;
I 's off ut put owr exin's in,
    An' git it deeun at yance.
Cūm! gi' 's a kiss o' t' heead on 't,
    An' meeak na meear ut du;
My hand 's here, wi' my heart in 't,
    Tak' them beeath—thou s' niver rue!

OXENFELL DOBBY.

A Reminiscence of Langdale.

ACCOMPANIED by the holder of a small farm in the dales, I was once riding up Yewdale sometime beyond the middle of a winter night. The fields on our right and the slopes and ledges of the screes and fells to the left and in front were shrouded in a vestment of frozen snow, which glared under the starlight with a brilliancy of reflection that rendered the absence of the moon unnoticed and uncared for. But the scattered groves and coppices to the eastern side, and the perpendicular craggs elsewhere, on neither of which the snow could rest as it fell, stood out black and dismal—blotches sable on a field argent —(queer heraldry this, but so suggested)—with an intensity of gloom, a weird dreariness of aspect, which may hardly be realized by those who have looked upòn Yewdale only when arrayed in the light verdure of spring, the matured leafiness of summer, or the marvellous variegation of autumn, under any one of which conditions that fair vale may fairly claim pre-eminence in beauty over all other minor dales of the Lake country.

On the occasion I tell of, the solemn desolation of the scenery, and the oppressive silence, broken only by the quick tramp of our ponies' feet on the crisp snow, combined to discourage all thought of conversation or remark; and we traversed the whole length of the vale without the interchange of sentence or word. When, however, we had reached the point where the road to Tilberthwaite and Langdale Head diverges from that to Skelwith, and I was about to follow the latter, my companion laid his hand upon my rein, and said, in a rather peremptory tone, "We s' teeak t' tudder rooad, if yee pleease;" and on my objecting to quit the smoother and shorter road for the longer and rougher, he persisted—" It may bee as yee say, beeath t' better an' t' bainer, bit nowte wad hire me to teeak t' rooad ooer Oxenfell at this hour o' t' neet, an' that's o' about it." "But why?" I remonstrated, disinclined to yield in a matter of such importance to reasoning like this. "I s' tell yee why," he replied, "when we's seeaf at my awn fireside, if ye sud ha'e time ut lissen." "Is it a story?" I asked with some interest. "It's nowte mitch of a stooary," said he, "bit what ther's on't 's true, an' that's meear ner can be said for many a better stooary. Bit cūm on, an' ye s' happen hear." I resisted no longer, and we pursued our journey through Tilberthwaite, where the piebald dreariness of the scenery was even more marked and more depressing than in Yewdale. We reached our destination without disaster, but not without danger. The broad, deep ford in the stream, which there divides the two counties, and which we had to cross, was edged on either bank by a high, abrupt shelf of strong ice, very dangerous to slidder off, and very difficult to scramble upon. Indeed, my fellow traveller, with his rough, clumsy little steed, more accustomed to the *stangs* of muck-cart or peat sledge than to saddle work, had a roll on the farther side—luckily rolling towards the land, and not into the water. But my sagacious old "Targus," who, as I was wont in those days to boast, could carry me over any ground on which a mountain goat or a Herdwick sheep could find a foot-hold, after testing the strength of each slippery ledge by a heavy paw or two, traversed the dangerous passage with the same steadiness with which I had known him pace over others where a slip or a stumble would have had much more serious results.

Seated comfortably at the grateless peat fire of my travelling companion, now my host, and assured of the probability of leisure to hear his story out, I reminded him of the condition under which he had induced me to take the longer and less practicable way to his fell-girt house; and after some coy deprecation, which sat awkwardly enough upon his homely features and dale nurtured manner, he began.

"Jūst about ten year syne, of jūst sic anudder neet as t'is, only t' snā' wasn't frozzen, I was out efter t' yārs." "Poaching?" I interpolated. "Co't as yè like," said he, in a tone of indifference. "I was out efter t' yārs. I'd gitten a yār or two ooer about Holme grūnd way, an' I was meeakin' heeam alang t' rooad atween Hodge Clooas an' Oxenfell Cross, when I thowte I was gā'n ut meet sūm fellows I cud heear toakin', bit cudn't see. Ye knā', t' rooad's o' heets an' hooals theear about, an', for that reeason, I dudn't think mitch o' nit seein' 'em; bit whoaiver they med be, I dudn't want them ut see *me*. Sooa I gat ooer t' steean fence wi' t' gun an' t' yārs, an' croodel't doon aback on't ut let 'em git whyetly by. Well, they com on, an', as I cūd hear, they wor fratchin cruelly o' t' way as t'ey com. Ther' was two on 'em, plain aneeuf, for sùm'times yan spak', an' sùm'times anudder, an', gaily oft, they beeath spak' at yance. As they co' narder till whār I was hidin', t' fratch gat feurcer an' louder ner iver, an' they shoutit, t' yan ooer t' tudder, whedder ut shout t' harder; bit for o' that, I cudn't meeak out a wūrd 'at they said. When they gat ebben fornenst me, yan o' them let out a meeast terrable skrike, an' I lowpt back ooer t' wo' ut seeav life. *Ther' was neàbody theear!* They wor rooarin' an' screeamin' wi'in six yirds o' mè, as I streetent mysel' up ut lowp t' wo', an' when I gat to me feet o' t' tudder side ther' was nowte! An' meear ner that, ther' wasn't a feeut-mark i' t' snā' bit my awn, an' they co' t' tudder wày. How I gat heeam wi' my gun an' my yārs I knà'n't, an' I niver mun knā'—bit when I wācken't i' t' mooernin' theear was t' gun an' yārs atop o' t' teeable, an' theear was I i' my bed.

"An' now I've telt yé t' reeason 'at I wodn't cū' heeam by Oxenfell Cross. I niver hev been, 'cept i' dayleet, on t' rooad whār them fellows woaks, an' I niver will, sa lang as I can git anudder 'at's less nor a scooer o' miles about."

"Then is that road said to be haunted?" I enquired. "*Said* to be hā'ntit!" he exclaimed, in a tone of wonder and contempt. " Whār ha'e yee been o' yer life, if yé hevn't hard o' Oxenfell Dobby?" "Has it been seen by any one besides you?" "Ey," replied he, "by hunderts o' fooak! Why, bless yé! āld Ben Grave gat seckan a torn as he was cūmin' heeam yance leeat frae Hāks'ed fair, 'at he dūd na meear gūd. He niver wod tell what it was, bit ivery body was suer 'at it was flayin' o' sūm mak', an 'a varry sairious mak' tu, for, as I said, āld Ben niver dūd no meear gūd efter that neet—bit dwinet away an' deet."

"Is it known," I asked, "how the place came to be haunted?" "Why! It *is*—partly. It's knā'n an' it isn't knā'n as a body may say—bit I can tell yé o' 'at's knā'n about it, if yé like ut hear." "Tell away then," said I, "I like to hear." "Well!" he again began, "Ya Kersmas, afooer I can mind, ther' was a hake aboot Clappersgeeat, an' ther' was a stranger at it 'at varry few knà't owte about—bit it seeun gat out 'at he was a new Scotch gardener 'at hed just cūm't tull Rydal Ho'. As t' neet went ooer fooak nooatisht 'at he was girtly teean up wi' lile Betty Briggs—a lively, rooesy-cheek't bit of a winch 'at com' frae Tilberthet. Betty hed an āld sweetheart theear 'at they co't Jack Slipe; bit she was sa pleeas't wi' t' new an' 'at she wodn't hev owte ut say tull Jack. It was plain aneeuf tull o' theeear 'at he dudn't hoaf like't; an' when t' Scotchman kiss't Betty i' t' cushion dance, t' fooak aside o' Jack cūd hear his teeth crack as he grūnd 'em togidder.

"When t' dance brak' ūp t' gardener wod see Betty heeam, an' as Betty hed nowte ut say ageean it, they set off togidder up t' rooad alang t' Brathay —an' Jack Slipe follow't by his-sel' a gay bit behint 'em.

"T' Scotch gardener niver co' back tull Rydal Ho'. He was niver seen ageean wi' neàbody. He partit wi' Betty at her fadder duer i' Tilberthet— she said—an' that was t' last on him!" "And was nothing ever heard of him?" I enquired. "Why! nowte 'at was owte. Theear was a hoaf silly lass about Chapel-Steel 'at said she'd hed t' Scotchman' heead iv her brat ya meeunleet neet—bit when she was teean up an' quees't about it, they cūd meeak nowte out on her, an' they let her lowce. It *was* said 'at Jooahn Tūrner, 'at hed t' Oxenfell farm afooar Grave fooak, fund t' beeans of a Christian yance when he was cūttin' a drain iv his pastur', bit it was niver leuk't intull, an' Jooahn said lile about it."

"And what about Jack Slipe?" "Well! queerly aneeuf, he weddit t' lass 'at dūd o' t' mischief, an' dee't afooar he was an āld man, leeavin' Betty wi' a yūng family. He was niver knà'n ut smile or teeak part iv any spooart. He ol'a's hed a wild scār'tly leeuk: as he woak't alang a rooad he keept glimin' fūrst ooer t' ya shou'der an' than ooer t' tudder, an' he niver durst bide by his-sel' efter t' darkenin'. He leev't sarvant for a while wi' āld Jooasep Tyson of Yakrow, an' wheniver āld Joo'ep seed any o' them signs of a bad conscience, he wod say, 'Cūm! Dyne the', Jack, thou med as gūd confess. Thou knā's thou dud it!' Bit whedder Jack dud it or nit neàbody can tell for suer. An' that's t' way it mun rist!"

MEENIE BELL.

WULL ye meet me, Meenie Bell? Wull ye
tryste yince mair wi' me?
Where the sauchs half hide the burnie as
it wimples on its way?
When the sinking sun comes glentin' through the
feathery birken tree,
Till ye'd trow a thousand fairy fires wer' flichterin'
on the brae.

Wull ye meet me, Meenie Bell? Wull ye say ye'll
meet me there?
An' come afore the gloamin' fa's to hear what I've
to tell?
For I'm gaun away the morn, an' I'll weary lang
an' sair
'Or I see ye're bonnie face again—sae meet me,
Meenie Bell!

Meenie Bell.

I'll be far away frae Middlebie for monie an' monie
    a day;
An' I want ae curl o' gowden hair to treasure
    evermore.
I've a keepsake braw for you, an' I've something
    mair to say—
Aye! a hantle mair to tell ye than I've ever tellt
    afore.

Thus I fleech't wee Meenie Bell till her heart grew
    soft an' kin'
An' she met me near the burnie as the simmer
    gloamin' fell;
We pairtit or 'twas day, an' o' a' the nichts I min'
The brichtest in my mem'ry is that nicht wi' Meenie
    Bell.

I thocht her heart was troth-fast, but my image
    faded oot,
An' a stranger took the place in't that she said she'd
    keep for me;
For time gaed creeping on, an' her hopes changed
    into doobt,
An' doobt to caul' mistrustin', while I toilt ayont
    the sea.

I've warselt wi' the worl' weel—I've run a wunnin'
   race,
But, aih! I'm of'en wushin' when I maunder by
   mysel',
An' a' my weary strivin's through lang lanesome
   years I trace,
I had bidden puir i' Middlebie and mairiet Meenie
   Bell.

"A LOCKERBYE LYCKE."[1]

(MODERN ANTIQUE.)

Ye've aiblins heard o' Wullye Smyth,
    Ane hosteler wychte was he ;
Quha wonn't at the sygne o' the bonnie Black Bull,
    I' the toon o' Lockerbye.

For Wullye, he drawyt the best o' wyne,
    An' brewyt the best o' yelle,
An' mixyt the best o' brandye punch,
    As neebour Lairds coulde telle.

For aft the neebour Lairds conveent
    At Wullye's to drynke theyre wyne,
An' hech ! quhan they yokyt the brandye punch,
    They raysyt ane unco schyne.

"A Lockerbye Lycke."

An! ance, on the nychte o' a huntan' tryste,
    A blythesome companye
There lychtyt doon i' the Black Bull closse,
    Wychte Wullye's wyne to pree.

An' there war Johnstones an' Jardines routh
    Amang that rattlan' crewe,
Wi' Herbert Herryes o' fayre Ha' Dykes,[2]
    An' his buirdlye byllye Hughe;

An' gallaunte Wullye o' Becks was there,
    Wi' Wullye o' Kyrtletoone :*
Sae they byrl't awaye at the reid, reid wyne,
    As the toasts gaed roun' an' roun'.

Whyle up an' spak wylde Wullye o' Becks,
    An' theyre fusionless toasts he curst,
"We'll toom a glasse tylle ilk man's lasse,
    An' Ha' Dykes maun name his first!"

Than up gatte the Laird o' bonnie Ha' Dykes—
    "Weel! rayther nor marre fayre myrthe,
Here's wynsome Jean o' the Wylye Hole,
    The flower o' Tundergayrthe;

---

* Friends of the author introduced anachronically, as also is Wullie Smyth, who flourished at Lockerbie during the author's "school-day time."

"A Lockerbye Lycke."

"An' he quha wunna drynke fayre to thatte
    Maun quytte thysse companye;
An' he quha lychtlyes thatte sweet lasse,
    Maun answer it weel tylle me."

Then up spak' Wullye o' Kyrtletoone,
    (A sleekye deevil I trowe,)
"Folke say, up the Water o' Mylke, that she lykes
    Ye're byllye farre better nor yowe!"

The reid marke brunt on the Herryes his bree,
    An' wow but he lookyt grymme:
"Can ye thynke that the flower o' the Mylke suld
    bloom
For a beggarlye loon lyke hymme?

"Can ye thynke that ane haughtye dame lyke her
    Coulde looke wi' a kyndlye e'e
On ane quha for everye placke that he spens,
    Or wastes, maun som on me?"

"An' div ye thynke," cryet the wrathfu' Hughe,
    "It's noo my turne to speer—
That ever a leal heartyt lassie could lo'e
    A sumph for the sake o' his gear?

"An' div ye thynke"—mayre scornfu' wordes
  Younge Hughe essayet to speake,
But his brither's rychte han' rase high in wrathe,
  An' fell on his lowan' cheeke.

Than doon at that wanbritherly strayke
  Dyd Hughe the Herryes fa',
An' for to redde this fearsome fraye,
  Uppe lappe the gentles a':

An' auld Wullye Smyth cam toytlan' benne—
  "Quhat's wrang amang ye noo?
It's a wonnerfu' thynge that 'sponsible menne
  Maun fechte or they weel be fou."

Fu' slawlye did Hughe Herryes ryse,
  An' the never a worde he sayde,
But he gloom't an' he tore his gluve wi' his teeth,
  As furthe frae the room he gaed.

He muntyt his gude grey meare i' the closse,
  An' he gallopyt aff lyke wudde.
"Eh, sirs!" quo' auld Wullye Smyth, "Eh, sirs!
  This never maun come tille gude;
For quhan ever a Herryes he chows his gluve,
  It's ane earnest o' deidlye feud!"

· · · · ·

"A Lockerbye Lycke." 103

That myrthsome band they tynte theyre myrthe,
    The gude wyne tynte its power,
An' ilke man glower't at his neebour's face
    Wi' a glum an' eerye glower.

The Herryes he lootyt his heid to the board,
    I' sorrowe but an' shame;
The lawin' was ca't—ilk took tille his horse,
    An' sochte his ain gate hame.

Kynde Wullye o' Becks sayde lowne tille his frien',
    We maun ryde Ha' Dykes his way;
But the Herryes owreheard, an' shook his heid,
    An' doolfu' did he saye—

"Alane! alane! I maun dree my weirde
    For the deede this nychte saw dune;
But O that the palsye had wuther't my han',
    Or it strooke my fayther's sonne!"

    .   .   .   .   .

Atweest Ha' Dykes an' the Water o' Mylke
    Rosebanke lies half-waye doone,
An' Chayrlye Herryes laye there that nychte,
    An' he was sleepyn' soune.

Quhyle he was rousyt i' the howe o' the nychte
    Wi' a dynne at his wundow board,
For his youngest bryther was dunneran there
    Wi' the hylte o' a sheenless sworde.

Sayan', "Chayrlye, I've mayde ye a Laird the nychte,
    An' I maunna be here the morne,
My blade is barken't wi' Herbert's blude,
    An' he lyes at Hurkelle Burne."

He muntyt his meare i' the fayre muinlychte,
    An' he pryckyt out owre the greene,
But never agayne in Annandale
    Was blythe Hughe Herryes seene.

Na! never agayne i' Dry's'al' Kyrke,
    Norre ever atte Lockerbye fayre,
The lasses quha lo'ed the blynke o' his e'e,
    Saw that blythe e'e-blynke mayre.

There was some folke sayde that his wynsome corse
    I' the fathomless sea was sunke;
Some sayde he was slayne i' the German wars—
    An' some that he deet a monke.

    .   .   .   .   .

"A Lockerbye Lycke."

Quhanne Chayrlye Herryes had ca't his menne,
    I' dool but an' i' frychte ;
He boun't him awaye to Hurkelle Burne,
    An' saw ane awfu' sychte.

For there the chief o' his aunciente house
    I' waesome plychte did lye,
Wi' his heid on the banke, his feet i' the burne,
    An' his face to the sternye skye.

Ane hastye batte wrochte unco chaynge ;
    Younge Chayrlye noo was Lairde,
An' Herbert layde i' the Herryeses aysle,
    I' Dry's'al' auld Kirk-yayrde.

But fearfu' sychtes hae beene seene sinsyne,
    An' monye a late-gaune wychte
Quhan stayveran' hame by Hurkelle Burne,
    Hes gotten a lyfe-lang frychte.

A voice ilke year as that nychte comes roun',
    Yells a' the plantyns throo—
"*There never was Herryes that dreet a strayke,*
    But he garr't the smyter rue."

An' what has been seen I downa telle,
  But this I ken fu' weel
That rayther nor cross that burne at e'en,
  There's monye wad face the deil.

An' ance quhan I was a smayke at the schule,
  I was late on Lockerbye Hylle,
An' sure o' a flyte quhan I ance wan hame,
  I gaed wi' lyttle gude wylle;

But thynkinge on monye a fayre excuse,
  Juste aung-er awaye to turne,
I'd got a rychte feasible storye framyt,
  As I loupit owre Hurkelle Burne.

Quhan somethynge rase wi' ane eldrytche skrayche,
  An' a deevylyshe dynne it mayde,
As doon the burn whyrre! whyrre! whyroo!
  Lyke a flaughte o' fyre it gaede.

My hayre lyftit up my cap frae my heide,
  Cauld sweite ran owre my bree,
The strengthe was reft frae my trummelan' lymbs,
  An' I cower't upo' my knee.
'Twas ane horryble thochte to forgayther wi' ghaysts,
  Quhan I'd just been coynan' a lee.

"A Lockerbye Lycke."

But awaye belyve like a troute frae a gedde,
    Or a maukyn frae yammeran' tykes,
I fledde nor styntyt to breathe or looke backe,
    Quhyle I wan to the bonnie Ha' Dykes.

My tale was tauld. They leuche, an' quo' they,
    "A frychtyt pheasaunte spryngs
Wi' a skraich an' a whyrre;"—but I threepyt them doone,
    That I kenn't it was nae sic thyngs,
For quhatte could pit me i' sic mortal dreide
    That flees upo' mortal wyngs?

The gyrse growes greene about bonnie Ha' Dykes,
    On meadowe, brae an' lea;
The corn waves wyde on its weel wrochte rygges,
    An' its wuddes are fayre to see.

Its auld Ha' house 'mang the chestnut trees
    In statelye beautye stan's;
But I wadna gaen backe by the burne that nychte
    For Ha' Dykes an' a' its lan's.

NOTES.

1. This phrase is generally applied to a heavy back-handed blow. It is said to have originated at the battle of Dryfesands, which was fought near to Lockerbie in 1593, between the Nithsdale and the Annandale clans, the former being defeated with terrible slaughter. It was found after the battle that many of the slain had been killed by a slashing sword cut across the face, from a blow peculiar to the Johnstones, and hence called the "Lockerbye lycke."

2. Halldykes, in the parish of Dryfesdale, Dumfriesshire, where the writer passed some years of his boyhood, was formerly the seat of a branch of the Herries family; and, with three or four adjacent farms, formed almost the last remnant of their large border estates held by the descendants of that anciently powerful and noble house; one member of which is immortalized as the builder of the Tower of Repentance, and another as Queen Mary's "loyal and brave Lord Herries!" Sir Robert Herries, founder of the great London banking house of Herries, Farquhar, and Co., and the Right Hon. J. C. Herries, once Chancellor of the Exchequer, were both scions of the old stock of Halldykes. Like most old family seats in the same district, Halldykes possesses, numerically speaking, a highly respectable corps of bogles (as the writer knew to his great and frequent tribulation); the origin and mode of developement of one of the most prominent of which is related pretty faithfully, according to local tradition, in the preceding rhyme.

"THE FARMERS' WIVES O' ANNANDALE."

Being shown, at Lockerbie, a printed programme of after-dinner proceedings at the celebration there of Mr. R. Jardine's marriage, the writer noticed in the list the sentence that heads this page, and enquired if it were a toast or a song. When told it was the former, he said it deserved to be a song; and, acting on his own hint, crooned out the following verses on his homeward journey by rail.

The farmers' wives o' Annandale!
   Gude haud them bein an' braw;
Ilk rules within her foothy hame,
   Like leddy in her ha'.
Ilk yearns to guide her ain gudeman
   Wi' love that downa fail;—
They irr the wale o' woman-kind—
   The wives o' Annandale!

The farmers' wives o' Annandale!
   I've kent their gates fu' lang;
They're worthy weel the wine cup's grace—
   Weel worthy o' a sang.

But ne'er to tell their worth aricht,
    May toast or sang avail;
They far transcend a' rhymin' skill—
    The wives o' Annandale!

The farmers' wives o' Annandale
    Shew fine at kirk an' fair;
But see them at their ain firesides—
    They shine the brichtest there.
Wi' gracious smiles an' winsome words
    The stranger guest they hail;
They're angels in a hamely sphere—
    The wives o' Annandale!

The farmers' wives o' Annandale!
    They strive frae morn till nicht,
Without, within, through but an' ben,
    To haud a' rowin' richt;
To keep contentit their gudemen,
    Their bairnies feal an' hale,
Till baith rise up an' ca' them blest—
    The wives o' Annandale.

The chiel' that hes in Annandale
    A weel-waled farm an' wife,
Has drawn twae glorious prizes frae
    The lucky-bag o' life.

An' may they prosper, stock an' store,
  In ever hichtinin' scale,
Whae treasure in their hames an' hearts
  The wives o' Annandale.

A REMINISCENCE OF CORRIE.

Of a' the streams o' Annandale
    Wi' names embalm't i' sang or story,
Gin Mylke for beauty, beer the bell,
    1 think I'd gi'e the mell to Corrie.

It's "up Corrie—doon Dryfe,"
    (Gin a coortin' ye wad toddle)
"That's the gate to seek a wife"—
    (Hoo daft aul' rhymes bide in yin's noddle!)

But sud ye take ye're way by Corrie,
    'Till ye come gey near to Borelan',
Ye'll aye see muir an' bent afore ye—
    Scarce ochte a' roon' but bent an' muirlan'.

"There's Corrie Lea an' Corrie Law—
    Corrie Mains—an' mowdies hork" there—
"Corrie Hill an' Corrie Ha'—
    Corrie Common, Corrie Kirk" there.

A Reminiscence of Corrie.

But Corrie Kirk's nae kirk ava—
   Corrie Hill's nae hill to roam on—
Snell's the blast on Corrie Law—
   Scant the gerse on Corrie Common.

They tell me Corrie's alter't now;
   It's drain't, they say, an' fenced an' plantit;
But as I min' 't, lang syne, I trow,
   Drain, fence, an' biel war sairly wantit.

Than what is't gars me ply my pen
   I' scribblin' doon this rhymin' clatter?
An' what is't mak's me aye sae fain
   To hear or read o' Corrie Water?

Atweel it is a simple thing
   As ever dreamer wastit time on;
Scarce worth the while to say or sing—
   For this is what I'm boun' to rhyme on :—

The mem'ry o' a denty quean,
   I couldna draw a plain-spak' word frae;
Scarce heard ava—no fairly seen—
   An' never efter seen or heard frae.

A Reminiscence of Corrie.

A' day we'd stey't at Corrie Common,
    Drinkin', thrawin' quoits, an' jeerin';
An' doon to Stidriggs, or the gloamin',
    Five wil' chiel's we gaed careerin'.

(Jock Porteous, An'ro Hen'erson,
    Wull Fergyson, me, Wullie Beaty.
Twae, like mysel', may yet leeve on—
    The ither twae—Aih me, the pity!)

But passin' by a wee cot-house,
    Wi' riggin' laigh, an' gable suety,
Yin cries oot sae baul' an' croose,
    "Come, boys, c' way in, an' licht the cutty!"

I'd maist ill tricks a lad can ha'e—
    An' *some I hadna neebors spak o'*—
But naither frien' nor foe could say
    I ever cared to blaw tobacco.

An' in they gaed; but I stood there
    Before the door, a tentless sentry,
Till startled by a vision fair
    Gaun jookin' ben across the entry.

A Reminiscence of Corrie.

Blate—blate an' backwarts aye I've been,
　An' niver forrat-ways nor saucy.
But where's the guff at bricht nineteen
　'At wadna chace a fleein' lassie?

Sae ben I slinkit—hat i' han'—
　An' there, beside the wee bit wunnock,
I saw a peerless maiden stan',
　Just pantin' like a hare i' panic.

Wi' shapely form i' braw black silk—
　Lang curls as black's the silk, an' blacker—
A changefu' cheek—a throat like milk:
　An' lown an' pawkily I spak' her.

I pled for my companions rouch—
　I trow't they couldna mean to fley her:
But only heard her breath's quick souch,
　For fient a word could I get frae her.

I howp't she didna think *me* rude—
　Civility I weel intendit;
An', quit I naither wad nor could,
　But pardon—gin I *had* offendit.

I ventur't yince to speir her name—
   I offen askit where she cam' frae—
(That hoosie boodna' be her hame)
   An' thochte I heard ae word like *Wamphray*.

But plague licht on thae rantin' chiel's,
   'At couldna let yin coort i' quayet,
But keepit cryin'—bletherin' de'ils !—
   "Hoy! This is no the bit to stey at;

Co' way to Stidriggs!"—sae I gaed,
   But first the lassie low I herkit,
"I'll come again?" was what I said—
   An' nae denial I remerkit.

We wan to Stidriggs Bent—but haith!
   Our *bent* was Stidriggs' tea an' toddy;
An' he that wadna roose them baith,
   Maun be a puir wanwauchtie body.

To Whitcastles I should ha'e gaen,
   But weet!—I've seldom seen the like o' 't—
An' An'ro swore i' siccan a rain
   He wadna turn a gangrel's tyke out.

A Reminiscence of Corrie.

Twae close box-beds, to five big chiel's,
    Presentit scrimp accommodation;
But, "heids an' thraws, or necks an' heels,"
    They'd haud by An'ro's invitation.

As they begood to think o' bed,
    An opportunity I grippit,
Borrow't, no askin', some ane's plaid,
    An' furth into the rain I slippit.

An' though the gate I hardly kent,
    I' trustfu' love's instinct confidin',
I, darklin', stayvelt owre the bent,
    An' fan' the cot, but ither guidin'.

An' nearin' that wee hoose at last,
    O' monie a fletherin' wordie thinkin',
I saw, what gar't my heart beat fast,
    A licht frae oot its window blinkin'.

I keekit through, but nochte could see;
    A claith was there, half drawn, half drappit;
But sure the licht was meen't for me;—
    Upon the glass I lichtly chappit.

An' seun I heard the openin' door;
   An' through its chink I saftly glidit;
But turnin' on the lichted floor,
   I saw I'd been sair, sair misguidit—

I saw what gar't my heart stan' still,
   An' set my verra flesh a' creepin',
While doon my limbs the sweit draps chill,
   Like thowin' snaw gaed dreepin', dreepin'.

    •

I' place o' braw black silken goon—
   A bed-goon an' a drogget coatie;
I' place o' ringlets clusterin' doon—
   A reekit mutch an' chaft-locks tawtie;

I' place o' saft lid-droopin' e'en—
   Ae wulcat spark—a winkin' won'er;
I' place o' lips wi' bliss atween—
   Twae gums wad gar a corby scunner;

I' place o' broo an' throat o' sna'
   An' bosom fraucht wi' sweet emotion—
A face an' figur' 'passin' a'
   The gruesomeness o' earth or ocean.

An' sic a tongue—Gude guide a' weel!—
   She lows't on me—sic fearfu' flytin'!
I' sic a voice—half craik, half squeel—
   Wi' jeers an' jibes braid, bitter bitin'.

"To gie yin fash," Rob Burns declared,
   "An aul' wife's tongue's a feckless matter,"
But honest Robin never heard
   That aul' wife's tongue i' Corrie water.

An' whan she made a calmer souch,
   An' stey't a wee her skirlin' ang-er,
I heard, far ben, a sweet wee lauch,
   An' dowdna thole the ordeal lang-er.

I flang the carlin fierce aside,
   An' left her up hersel' to gether;
An', frae her cot, wi' wrathfu' stride,
   I fled to face the midnicht w'ather.

An' back I took my darksome way,
   By gerse grown-dykes an' resh-rouch heid rigs;
By spretty knowe an' staney brae,
   An', sair forfowch'en, wan to Stidriggs,

A Reminiscence of Corrie.

Where, hingin' up the borrow't plaid,
  An' owre my queer mischanter smilin',
I took my share o' ae box-bed,
  But couldna sleep for thochte's beguilin'.

For whae could yon sweet lassie be
  That lauch't at that aul' carlin' scaul'in'?
'Twas plain, I've said afore, to see
  That cot-hoose couldna be her dwallin'.

How cam' she to be wonnin' there
  I' that aul' muirlan' clay-wa't biggin?
How could a gem sae bricht an' rare
  Be treasur't 'neath its crazy riggin'?

It's mair nor therty year sin syne—
  That maiden's aiblins noo a grannie—
But 'mang the folk I like to min',
  I offen see her, skeich an' bonnie.

An' whiles I've thochte that hed she gi'en,
  An' keep't, her word to be sweet-heartit,
Like ither sweethearts, she'd ha'e been
  Frae mem'ry's hauld lang, lang depairtit.

A Reminiscence of Corrie.

For weel I wat, fair favours won
   Ha'e frae men's minds aye seuner slippit
Nor ochte we've set oor hearts upon,
   An' triet to grip—but fail't to grip it.

REMINISCENCES OF LOCKERBIE.

Aul' Lockerbie! aul' Lockerbie! the dear wee toon to me!
Where, never fleyed, a boy I played, an' roved a younker free,
Wi' heart sae licht that life was bricht as never mair it shall,
For never mair I'll ramble where I drank o' Bessie's wal'.*

Yes! dear to me is Lockerbie, its houses wee an' big,
Its "Up the gate," its "Doon the gate," its "Cross," an' "Through the brig,"

---

* Bessie's Well was not far from the foot of "Cuddie's Lane." The writer has been informed that the well was drained or filled up by operations connected with the formation of the railway. This ancient fountain, the destruction of which is to be deplored, had the traditional reputation of attaching all who drank of it with a lasting affection to the town of Lockerbie. Bessie's Well has been restored and enclosed (1872).

Its closes mirk,* its stumpy kirk, its fu' an' thrang kirkyard,
Where caul' an' deep some dreamless sleep I wish dour death had spared.

A hame to me was Lockerbie when half its roofs were theek,
An' jeests, an' jaums, an' gapin' lums, a' black-japann't wi' reek ;
Whan monie were the middens nerr the whunstane-causey't street ;
But cosie aye its hearthstanes lay afore the stranger's feet.

Than Lockerbie had sichts to see at race times an' at fairs,
Wi' Jocks an' Jeans, strang chiel's an' queans, i' scores an' scores o' pairs ;
An' gledging oot the roads aboot or the fair had weel begun,
We'd watch the braw, braw lasses a' pu' on their hose an' shune.

* The existence of "closes mirk" in Lockerbie may be disputed ; but the writer holds one or two in his recollection well suited to the taste of those who love the darkness rather than the light.

I wadna' gie aul' Lockerbie for ony toon I ken,
For kindly were the kimmers there, an' kindly too the men,—
Atweel the *bouk* were kindly folk, an' some were gey an' queer,
An' whilk remain an' whilk are gane I downa bide to spier.

My thochts oft flee to Lockerbie at midnicht's waukrife hour,
An' thickly flock aul' mem'ries back wi' heart upheesing power,
An' schulemates dear, an' sweethearts fair, an' frien's o' days lang fled,
I' shadowy train appear again like phantoms roun' my bed.

There was gude aul' Jeanie Kennedy, an' Jimmie Rule, the blin',
Whase fiddle's squeal we liket weel though't had nae tune but yin;
Lizzie Dobie, Winnie Stobie, Nickie Scott an' puir Jean Hine,
An' aul' John Kerr, a lamiter, a pawkie frien' o' mine.

Josie Weepers, Geordie Robison, Tam Bell, an'
   Cripple Peg,
An' the puir man nocknamed "Providence," whae
   whiles gaed oot to beg.
The Cameronian merchants twae, the wee yin an'
   the lang,
An' Sawney Beck, wi's aul' white heck that scarce a
   fit could gang.

There was roup-crier Awnro' Jimmison, whae hirplet
   in his walk,
An' Wullie Smith, a carle o' pith whae squeekit in
   his talk,
An' wi' a pow maist like a lowe the singin' nailer
   chiel,
An' droothy twuns, twae burniewun's, Bob Johnston
   an' Jock Steel.

Wullie Corrie, Sandy Moray, than a licht amang the
   Whigs,
An' hairy-faced Bill Vairy, wi' his wife gaun sellin'
   pigs,

Funny-speakin' Peggy Meekin, wi' the meetin' nose an' chin,
An' Robie Rule,* aul' noisy tule, whase drum made sic a din.

There was winkin' Sandy Linton, makin' peeries roun' an' fine
(Within his doors hoo monie hours o' merriment I min'),
The pistol-fittit cooper carle whase name was aye a myth,
An' the twae whase names were bye-words, Wullie White an' Michael Smith.

Wi' mony mae than I may say, but yin I'd like to name
(Gin I forget to him my debt, I'll hide my heid for shame,)
Wi' great respec', the maister stric', an' danglin' frae his claws,
His badge o' rule i' the thrang aul' schule, the weel-worn cutty tawse.

---

* The town drummer and bellman, one of whose functions was to parade the streets, drumming the lieges of Lockerbie to bed at ten p.m., and out of bed at six a.m.—a custom which some thought "more honoured in the breach than the observance."

Sweethearts a score I whyles rhyme ow'r—their
    names, Bell, Barb'ra, Bess,
Ann, Kirsty, Kate, May, Margaret, Jean, Georgie,
    Jamesie, Jess,
Johanna, Helen, Hannah, Agnes, Maries twae or
    three,
An' a pauchtie dame I'm sweir to name, the dearest
    yince to me.

But monie a day has passed away, ay, monie a lang
    dark year,
Sin I'd the chance o' smile or glance frae them lang
    syne sae dear,
An' hoo they've fared, whase lots they've shared, or
    where the hames they've blest,
May sometime be revealed to me—but noo it's just
    a mist.

My scheulmates! hoo *they're* sqaunder't noo, I haena
    words to say,
Some east away, some wast away, they a' gaed far
    away—
But what-for say they're wide away, or sunder't far
    abreed ?
When, weel I wat, it's waur be that, the feck hae
    lang been deid.

Aih me! aih me! aul' Lockerbie, my heart sinks
    cauld an' wae
At the doolfu' thocht o' changes wrocht sin I speel't
    Mount Ulzie's brae;
But aye I'm fain to see't again, an' aye I hope an'
    pray
To rest a wee at Lockerbie afore I'm ca't away.

YAN O' T' ELECT.

The following was most kindly sent to me by a gentleman well known in west Cumberland who has, from boyhood, been a keen and judicious observer of the peculiarities of thought and speech prevailing amongst his unsophisticated and unlettered neighbours ; and who has also favoured me with extensive contributions to my stock of anecdotes illustrating the humourous side of rustic life in our common county. This remarkable piece possesses a higher value than any of *my* dialect productions, amongst which it appears, as being the veritable words used by one speaking the Cumberland vernacular and nothing else ; and also as an exposition and powerful expression of the opinions on the doctrine referred to that prevails amongst his class, who are generally very matter-of-fact, and impatient of anything that transcends their power of apprehension or that goes beyond the grasp of their every-day sense. The old man's self-laudation, when put upon his mettle, is perhaps the most characteristic point in the sketch.

BOUT five or six years ago a gentleman entered a station of one of our local railways, and found the worthy station master (whose original occupation was that of a small Cumberland farmer,) in a state of great excitement.

He enquired the cause, and received a reply of which the following is a verbatim report, committed to paper immediately afterwards. We must premise that Dr.——— was a well known amateur preacher, —a really benevolent man, who did good in his way, but had no charity for the opinions of others, and was ever intruding his views and advice on all who came in contact with him, and believed all who differed from him destined to perdition. The extreme Calvinistic doctrine of election and reprobation was a perfect mania with him. On this occasion he was accompanied by his servant, a man of sleek aspect, who distributed tracts, etc., for his master.

"What's t' matter wi' mé? Wey, theear matter plenty! That Dr.—— com' here aboot hoaf an oor sen to tak' t' train. I was stan'in' at t' time aback o' t' ticket wole, an' what d'yé think he says; —he says, says he, 'Isaac, you are a very wicked old man, and will most certainly be damned; you are worse than Cass (then under sentence of death in Carlisle gaol)—you are worse than a murderer.' Says I, 'Me war' ner a murderer! What the sham' an' hangment d'yé mean be that?' Says he, 'I mean this, old man; it has been elected from the beginning that certain men shall be saved, and certain shall be lost. You are among the latter, and you will most certainly be damned.' Says I, 'An' what 'ill come o' you?' Says he, 'Oh, Christ elected me many years ago.' Then, says I, 'I think he meàd a varra feckless choice; but if it be sooa, I wad like to know what I've deùn 'at I's to be damned! I've been weddit abeun forty year, an' I've hed twelve barnes, an' I browte them o' up weel, an' I edicated them weel, an' they've o' turn't oot weel; I've wrowte hard o' me life, an' I niver wrang't a man oot of a ho'penny—what mair can a man deu?' Says he, 'Isaac, you might do much more, you might follow the teaching of the Bible; you might sell all you have and give it to the poor.' Says I, 'Sell o' 'at I hev an' give 't to t' poor! Is I to sell t' bed fray anonder me wife 'at she's sleept on for forty year? Is I to sell t' chair fray anonder her 'at she's sitten on for forty year, an' turn her oot intil a dike gutter? What kind o' religion is ther' i' that?' Says he, 'Oh, the Lord would provide for you.' Says I, 'The Lord provide for mé! Wad t' Lord finnd mé wid a new bed an' a new chair?— an' if he dud, I wad likely hev to sell them ower ageàn! Sell o' 'at I hev an' gi' 't to t' poor! Do *you* sell o' 'at *you* hev an' gi' 't to t' poor? I niver hard tell o' yé sellin' o' 'at you hev an' gi'in' 't to t' poor! They tell me you hev atween fowrteen an' fifteen hundert a year,—an' mebbee yé may, for owte I know, gi'e away—we'll say, a hunder't a year, an' that'll be t' ootside be a gay bit.—Do you co' that sellin' o' 'at *you* hev an' gi'n' to t' poor. I tell yè, you're a rich man, an' I's no'but a poor an', wi' a loosey ten shillin' a week to leeve on; bit, accordin' to what I hev, I consider mysel' to be beàth a nowbler an' a generouser fella ner you irr! Noo, theear a poor Irish family 'at leeves nar oor hoose, an' ivery week end we send them o' t' scraps o' meat an' 'taties 'at we ha'e left, forby udder things;—that's far mair, accordin' to what I've gitten, ner your hunder't a 'ear! You talk aboot me bein' damned. Noo, I's neea scholar, bit I've read t' Bible for o' that, an' I've read 'at theear two mak' o' fwok 'at 'ill be damned—yan's leears, an' t' tudder's hypocrites. Noo, I'll preùv 'at you're beàth. You're a leear for sayin' 'at I was war' ner a murderer i' Carlisle gaol, an' you're a hypocrite for sayin' seea when you knew you were leein'! I know hoo you mak' o' fwok argies—you reùt t' Scriptur' through an' through to finnd owte 'at suits yé, an' than ye throw o' t' tudder ower-bword. An' I tell you what, Mr.——, theear anudder thing 'at I've read in t' Scriptur's—I've read 'at theear to be a day o' judgment. Noo, you cháps say 'at it's o' settl't afoorhan' what's to cum on us, whoa's to be seàv't an' whoa's to be damned. You say you're to be seàv't an' I's to be damned. Noo, what's t' use of a day o' judgment if it's o' settl't afoorhan'! Ther' 'ill be nowte to judge aboot! I'll tell yé what, Mr.——, theear *will* be a day o' judgment, an' beàth you an' me 'ill ha'e to mak' oor appearance; an' I doon't know bit upon

Yan o' t' Elect.

the whol' I'll stan' full oot t' better chance o' t' two! An' what's t' use, I wad like to know, o' you gā'n an' preachin' i' that girt leàth o' yours of a Sūnday neet till a parshal o' taggelts, if it's o' fix't what's to come on them?' Says he, 'Old man, I perceive you are a child of the devil.' Says I, 'Wey, mebbee! Bit I'll tell you what, Mr.——, t' divvel hesn't two better frin's in o' Cummerlan' ner you an' that man o' yours—an' which on yé 's t' bigger neàv I's suer I can't tak' upon mysel' to say.' Just than t' train com' up, an' my gentleman slipes. Theear was a kind of a country chap stan'in' ootside, an' when t' train hed gone, he com' intil t' stashun hoose, an' says, says he, 'Is that yan o' thūr Methody chaps?' 'No,' says I, '*it's yan o' t' Elect!*'"

KEATY CURBISON'S CAT.

AN OALD, OALD STWORY.

KEATY Cūrbison' cat hed a whudderin' waow,
    A waow like a yowl, fit to freeten a man ;
An' t' leet iv it' e'e was a green glentin' lowe—
Iv it' *e'e*, we may say, for it no'but hed yan.
T' ya lūg hed been rovven, an' hung like a cloot,
    While t' tudder stack ūp like t' cockad' iv a hat ;
Lang whiskers like brūssles spread o' roond it' snoot—
    It wosn't a beauty—Keàte Cūrbison' cat !

Keàty Cūrbison' cat was a terror to t' toon—
    Till butt'ry an' pantry it may'd hed a kay.
Intil ivery hoose, ayder up t' geàt or doon,
    By air-wole or chimla it wūmmelt it' way.

Keàty Curbison's Cat.

For thievin' an' reàvin' 'twas war' nor a fox,
   Ther' wasn't a hen-hoose it hedn't been at;
Young chickens, an' geslins, an' pigeons, an' ducks
   Wer' "ghem, gā 'way tul't" to Keàte Cūrbison' cat.

Keàty Cūrbison' cat like a tiger wad feight;—
   When it' back was weel up an' o' ruddy for war
It wad lick a cur dog mair nor ten times it' weight,
   An' mongrels an' messans they dursn't cū nār.
It hed leet of a trap, an' ya feùt was teàn off,
   An' it' tail hed been dock't—but it dūdn't mind that,
It wad flee at owte whick 'at wad give it a lofe—
   A hero, i' hair, was Keàte Cūrbison' cat.

Keàty Cūrbison' cat hed of lives a lang lot—
   Yè ma' toak aboot nine—it hed ninety an' mair;
It was preùf ageàn puzzen or pooder an' shot—
   They hed buriet it yance, but it still dudn't care.
It was tiet iv a meal-bag an' flung into t' beck,
   But t' bag it brong heàm for it' mistress a brat,
Limpin', trailin' 't ahint it wi' t' string round it' neck—
   T' beck cūdn't droon Keàty Cūrbison' cat.

Keàty Cūrbison' cat browte oald Keàty to grief—
   Pooar body! she nowder was cūmly nor rich—
An' t' neybors aboot settlet doon to t' belief
   'At her cat was a divil an' she was a witch.

An' they said, "Let us swum her i' t' tarn," an
    they dud;
She swom a lāl bit, an' than droon't like a rat,
An' t' cat aboot t' spot swom as lang as it cūd;
    An' finish't at last was Keàte Cūrbison' cat.

NOTE.

I remember reading somewhere the story of one of the many old women so treated, in the wisdom of our ancestors, who was drowned while undergoing the common ordeal of being bound and thrown into deep water—and her cat, supposed to be her familiar spirit, swimming in circles over the place where she sank till it became exhausted and was also drowned. A story which made a lasting impression on my young imagination.

JOSEPH THOMPSON'S THUMB.

AN OLD HARRINGTON STORY.

Jwosep' Thompson leev't lang ūp at Harrin'ton
    toon,[1]
An' a weel to dee, throughly oald marrow was Joe,
Wid a neive like a neàf, an' a feàce like a moon,
An' a shap', standin' ūp, like a tee-tak-up-o'.

Jwosep' Thompson hed ola's been hearty an' stoot,
    But trūbble o' sūm mak's gay sarten to cūm,
An' when threescwore an' two he hed jūst coontit oot,
    He was terrably tyl't wid a gedderin' thūmb.

For it feister't an' wark't wid sa beàdless a stoon,
    'At rist he gat nin for't by neet nor by day;
But he rantit aboot, or he reàv't ūp an' doon,
    Fairly greànin' his life an' fwoke's patience away.

Ther' wer' pokey oald wives aboot Harrin'ton than,
    An' a varst of advice, o' free gratis, he gat;
But he gat nèa 'mends, dudn't pooar oāld man,
    An' he fail't varra sair iv his leùks an' his fat.

He seeken't at meat,—nay, he'd bowk at a speùn!
    An' his beùrd he let growe like a Turk or a gwoat,
An' he squeak't iv his toak like a fiddle oot o' teùn,
    An' like bags full o' nowte hung his britches an' cwoat.

But o' things they telt him Joe triet tūll his thūmb—
    Sec as cerat', an' yal-grūnds, an' turmets an' skarn,
Screàp't taties, an' 'bacca, an' pooder wid rūm,
    An' reùts 'at they raik't oot o' t' boddom o' t' tarn.

An' fegs, an' bog-unnion, an' blackberry buds,
    An' carrots, an' pūppies, an' teàdsteùls, an' sneels,
An' soave meàd wid rozzle an' meal boil't i' sūds,
    An' t' fat rwoastit oot o' beàth hag-wūrms an' eels.

An' strang reisty bakin, an' boil't cabbish skrūnt,
    An' broon seàp an' sugger, an' typstic, an' tar,
An' he keept an oald pūltess of o' mak's upon't,[2]
    Till Joe an' his thūmb warn't nice to cū' nār.

Joseph Thompson's Thumb. 139

It was o' nèa use—nūt a crūmb dūd he mend!
An' t' parson co' tūll him to pray an' to read,
An' whisper, "I say, Jwosep'! think o' thy end"—
But he wadn't—he thowte of a doctor asteed.

An' tul't' doctor he dreàv iv his car—thumb an' o'—
An' t' doctor said, "Well, my lad—off this mūn cūṁ!"
An' he haggelt an' cot at his pultess-bleach't po',
Till Joe was meàd shot of his mūrderin' thumb.

T' doctor lapt ūp his hand varra fewsome an' reet,
An' Joe, like a man, pait him weel for his job,
An', creùnin', "I's m'appen git sūm rist to-neet,"
Joggelt heàm, pleased as Punch, wid his thumb in his fob.

An' to t' wife says he, "Tak' 't to t' churchyard oot o' geàt,
An' bury 't whoar I'll lig mysel' when I dee."
An' she went wid a trooin an' lantern, leàt,
An' left it i' t' spot whoar Joe said it mud be.

Jwosep' to'k till his meat, for his hand mendit weel—
(He hed gud healin' flesh, an' fine natur', hed Joe,)[3]
He screàp't off his beùrd—he gev ow'r wid his squeel,
An' was gittin' as pūbble an' roond as a bo'.

But jūst when he thowte o' his trūbble was geàn,
  A pain com' ageàn, wār nor iver he'd fund,(4)
An' theear it keept burnin' an' bworin' i' t' beàn
  O' t' thumb 'at was buriet an' coald under t' grūnd.

Jwosep' went back to t' doctor, an' t' oald wicket teul
  H'ard his teàl, an' says he, wid a snūrt an' a gūrn,
"If thy thumb's i' t' churchyard, thoo pooar priest-
    bodder't feùl,
  Thoo ma' mak' thysel' suer while it bides it 'ill
    būrn."

He laid him sūm plaisters an' soav on his po',
  An' gev him sūm stuff to lig on tūl't at heàm;
But nowte putten on tul't gev easement tūll Joe,
  For t' būrnin' an' bworin' wer' iverly t' seàm.

An' it keept on sa bad, he tūrn't maffelt an' maiz't,
  An' sa wankle an' wake, 'at he to'k tull his bed,
Whoar, liggin' hoaf deid, ey, an' mair nor hoaf
    craiz't,
  He cūd think aboot nowte but what t' doctor hed
    said.

He triet nūt to speak on't—He knew 'twasn't reet,
  But it ola's beàd by him—his uppermor' thowte;
An' he yammer't at t' wife tull she went back at neet
  To dig ūp t' oald thūmb, an' brong't heàm iv a
    cloot.

Joseph Thompson's Thumb.

They laid it i' t' gardin, an' hoo 't com' aboot
    Nowder t' mistress nor t' parson cūd under-cum-
stand,
But sarten it was, fray that varra time oot,
    Sairy Jwosep' was bodder't na mair wid his hand.

But Jwosep' was niver ageàn his oald sel'.
    An' a questi'n com' ūp still whativer he tried,
"If a thùmb i' t' churchyard was sa bad, whoa cūd tell
    What a corp' pùtten in't o'togidder mūd bide!"

This he maddelt aboot ebben endways away—
    As lang as he breath't it was ola's his drone;
An' t' wife hed na peace till he gat her to say
    He sud lig by his-sel' iv a field o' the'r oan.

An' Jóe tiet her up till her wūrd iv his will,
    For theear suer aneuf when he dee't it was fūnd
'At he'd left o' tull hūr, no'but if she'd fulfil
    His craze ageàn liggin' i' consecrate grūnd.

An' Joe hed his way, for a square roughish steàn[5]
    By t' dike, i' t' Sco'-lonnin', at this varra day,
Tells whoar Jwosep' Thompson ligs whyet an' leàn—
    Keep us weel fray sec doctors as Jwosep's, I pray!

An' keep us, I pray, fray o' wild wicket toak,
  Bringan' bodder an' fashment tull oald an' tull yūng.
Jwosep' Thompson wad ristit wid Christian fwoke,
  If t' doctor he went tull hed hodden his tūng!

NOTES.

1. Harrington Town, the ancient village about half a mile inland, is so called in distinction from Harrington Harbour, the small sea-port, which is modern. The heiress of the family which took its name and title from Harrington was mother of the Lord Bonville and Harrington, brother-in-law to the king-making Earl of Warwick. The manor was forfeited by the attainder of Henry Grey, Duke of Suffolk, great-grandson of the said Lord Bonville, and father of Lady Jane Grey, and given by the Queen (Mary,) to the Curwens of Workington, who still hold it.

2. Should this compendium of topical applications seem at all overcharged, I would state that it consists of well known popular remedies, mostly of *some* use, and falls far short, whether in variety, extravagance, or repulsiveness of the multifarious nostra recommended by amateurs of the healing art in Cumberland and the adjacent counties. The "poultice of o' maks" is not, as its name seems to imply, a compound, but a simple substance, which it is unnecessary to indicate more distinctly than to mention that it was generally turned to when pleasanter applications had failed. I have frequently heard old people extol its virtues as a promoter of suppuration, but I trust its use may now be classed with the "many precious rites and customs of onr rural forefathers," which, as Wordsworth has said, "are gone or stealing from us."

3. This alludes to the popular belief, not altogether unfounded, that readiness in healing is connected with an easy disposition.

4. A delusion common enough after amputation.

5. The stone stood behind the hedge which on the western side fences the lane called Scaw-lonning, near High Harrington. When I last saw it in 1871, the subjoined inscription was quite distinct upon it—plainer, indeed, than any of similar date in the churchyard :—

"JOSEPH THOMPSON may here be found
Who would not lie in consecrated ground
Died May 13th 1745
Aged 63 when he was alive"

With the traditional account of the circumstances that caused this fancy of Joseph Thompson's, the details given in the rhyme coincide as closely as my recollection of a tale heard in boyhood enables me to make them.

Since the first appearance of this, however, another version of the matter has been reported to me by old friends near the spot—but inasmuch as it does not account so perfectly as the old story for Joseph's objection to ALL consecrated ground, I feel bound to abide by my first choice. The, to me, new story tells that Joseph Thompson annoyed the clerk in the church so seriously by repeating the responses in a voice that quite drowned his, that at length the said functionary exclaimed during service—"Is thoo t' clark, or is I t' clark? If thoo's t' clark, cūm up hèar, an' I'll cūm doon thèar!"—and, on Joseph's paying no attention to his appeal, supplemented it by assaulting him. The clergyman taking his clerk's side in the quarrel, Joseph Thompson declared he would never come near the church again, dead or alive, and kept his word.

I think that my version is the better, whichever may be the truer tale. I have further been told that the stone formerly stood in the centre of the field—and on the land coming into the possession of Mr. John Christian Curwen, the farmer waited upon that distinguished agriculturist to obtain permission to remove it to the hedge-side, and to plough the field. When he was told the history of the monument, and its inscription was recited to him, Mr. Curwen exclaimed, *more suo*, "*Would not lie in consecrated ground!* Then, plough him up! D—— him, plough him up!"

CURSTY BENN.

Cūrsty Benn of Under-Skiddaw
   Leev't on t' land whoar he was bworn ;
Eight-ty yacre, lea an' meedow—
   Forty, green-crop, seeds an' cworn.
Cūrsty' wife, a fewsome body,
   Brong him barnes, some nine or ten,
Menseful, meat-heàl, fat an' ruddy ;—
   "Whoar's their like?" said Cūrsty Benn.

Cūrsty hed ya mortal failin'—
   Whoa may say they've less nor that·?—
Rayder fond was he o' trailin'
   Off frae heàm an' bidin' leàt.
Fray Kes'ick Kit was ola's leàtish ;
   Hoo that com' t' wife gat to ken,
When i' t' market neets she'd nwotish
   Signs o' drink i' Cūrsty Benn.

Cūrsty' wife was kind an' canny,
   Nowder gi'en to flyte nor fret ;
" Weel aneùf," she said, " I ken he
   Mayn't be cured by sulks an' pet ;

But I moon't sit by an' see him,
  Gear an' grun' spang-hew an' spen',
I mūn gang till Kes'ick wi' him!"
  Nowte ageàn't said Cūrsty Benn.

When they dadg't away togidder,
  O' row't reet a canny bit;
Cūrsty, pleas't to market wid her,
  Tiped his pints, but dūdn't sit.
No'but for a bit it lastit—
  Sooa 't's been afoor an' sen!
When fwoke thowte she'd wiled him past it,
  Tull't ageàn went Cūrsty Benn.—

Tull't ageàn i' t' public-hooses,
  Whilk an' Cūrsty dūdn't care;
Adam Gill's, or Mistress Boose's,
  T' Yak, t' Queen's Heed, or t' Hoonds an' Hare.
Through them o' t' wife whiles went laitin'—
  Whiles, for hours an' hours an' en',
In their shandry sat she waitin',
  Coald on t' street, for Cūrsty Benn.

Ya' fine neet when leàt she gat him—
  Fairly fworc'd to flyte, t' poor deàm
Lowsed her tongue reet freely at him,
  While t' oald yoad went stammerin' heàm.

Cūrsty Benn. 147

Whietly Kit bore her clatter,
　Nea back-wūrd he'd gi'en her, when
T' mèar pu't up aside some watter;—
　"Drink, gūd lass!" says Cūrsty Benn.

Lang she dronk, an' lood she grūntit,
　Till a gay gud drain she'd hed;
Than as t' rwoad yance mair she frūntit,
　Cūrsty' wife tūll Cūrsty said—
"Sees t'e, min! that pooar oald mèar,
　When she's full, she's t' sense to ken;
Can't thoo tak' a pattren bee her—
　Drink an' deùn wi't, Cūrsty Benn?"

"Whey!" says Kit, "but tūrn that watter
　Intill yāll, wid udder yoads
Swattin' roond it—hoddin' at her—
　Tellin' her t' time mak's na odds—
Shootin' oot, 'Here's te the', Cūrsty!'—
　(Mèars is mèars—men's nowte but men!—
But I dūrst lay a pūnd 'at dūrst Ee,
　She'd sit on—like Cūrsty Benn!"

NOTE.

Of this anecdote different versions are current, and various localities are assigned to it—Scotch as well as English. I presume to consider, however, the Cumberland version, as given above, the best of all that have been given.

TOM RAILTON'S WHITE SPATS.

"SPATS?" said Tom, "Nay! I niver hed a par o' spats i' my life; but yance I'd as nār as a toucher gitten two par; an' I's tell ye hoo it com' aboot 'at I dudn't.

"Nūt varra lang efter we wer' weddit, an oald uncle o' t' wife's com' ower t' fell frae Ireby to see us, an' stop wid us a bit. Ya ebenin' when we wer' sittin' crackin' away roond t' fire, some way or udder oor toak happen't to tūrn on men-fwoke's driss, t' change o' fashions, an' sec like; an' oald uncle Geordie begon to brag 'at they used to driss far better when he was yūng nor they dūd than; an' by way o' clinchin' his teàl, he says, 'Can ye finnd me a smo' steàtsman's sūn noo-a-days 'at 'll worder six par o' white corduroy knee britches o' at yance!' 'Six par o' corduroy britches?' says I. 'Ey,' says he, 'corduroy britches, as white as drip!' 'Whey, no!' says I, 'I wadn't ken whoar to leuk for a fellow 'at wad git six par o' britches of any mak' o' at yance?' 'Well than,' says he, 'jūst rūb yer

Tom Railton's White Spats.

een clear, an' leùk hard to this side o' yer oan fire,' says he, 'an' ye'll see a fellow 'at beath wad an' dud git them! When I furst begon to ride efter t' hoonds,' says he, 'I gat six par o' white cword britches, an' two par o' top beùts. T' beùts was worn oot many a year sen, but I've t' six par o' britches yit, laid bye, an' for owte I know they're as white as iver.' Wid that our wife spak up—she thowte a vast mair aboot my leùks than nor she does noo—an' she says, 'Uncle George,' says she, 'will ye iver weear yer white britches agean!' 'Nay, my lass,' says he, 'I think my white britches days is gaily weel ower, but what o' that?' 'O, nowte,' says she, 'but I've a nwotion 'at Tom here wadn't misbecome white britches an' top beuts, when he's ridin' aboot; an' as they're o' nea use till yersel' noo, ye'd better send them ower till him.' 'Whe—e—ey!' says he, iv a dronin' soort of a way, 'Whey! Whey! but m'appen they willn't gang on him,' says he. 'O!' says she, 'but ye know we med mebbe let them oot a bit, an' mak' them gang on him.' 'Well, well,' says her uncle, 'I'll send him ya par on them to try, an' if they fit, an' he likes them, he may hev mair efter.' An' sure aneuf, when he went back heam ageàn, he sent a par on them ower, as he said, as white as drip; an' we beàth thowte he mud ha' been a parlish oald buck if he hed o' udder things to match when he gat sec a stock o' white britches.

Nowte wad sarra t' wife, when we'd leukt at them, but I mud try them on theear an' than, an' see hoo they fittit. We gat a terrible begonk when we fund 'at they wadn't gang on at o'. He was rayder a wizzent oald fellow than, an' he'd been a wizzent fellow when he'd geàn sproguein' aboot iv his white corduroys mebbe thurty year afoor, for t' knees on them, wid o' t' buttons lowse, wadn't come ower t' bo's o' my legs, an' what was warse nor o' t' tudder, ther was nowte left o' t' seam to let them oot wid. Sooa they wer laid bye be theirsel's at oor hoose, just as t' tudder five par on them wer liggin' laid bye togidder at Ireby.

A gay while efter that, when I'd forgitten o' aboot t' white britches, an oald crony o' mine chanced to be iv oor part, an' co't to see us, an' stopt o' neet. We nwotish't 'at he hed shoes on, an' t' bonniest spats we'd iver owder on us seen; for they fittit roond his ancles an' ower his shoe tops widoot ayder a lirk or a lowse spot; an' I said, 'Charley,' says I, 'whoariver did tè manish to git sec fitters as them?" 'O!' says he, 'I hed t' pattren on them frae Scotland, an' my sister maks them for me as I want them.' 'Thy sister maks them!' says I, 'Whey, I wad ha' sworn thoo'd been to t' varra heid tailior i' Whitehebben for them!' 'Well,' says he, 't' pattren's sa plain an' simple 'at she cuts them oot by it, an' mak's them quite easy; an', as ye say, they fit as weel as if t' best tailior i' t' land hed been at t' makin' on them. But if ye like, I'll send ye t' pattren by post, an' Mistress Railton may try her hand at them for thee.'

"Well, t' pattren o' t' spats com, as Charley promish't it sud, an' efter she'd leùk't it weel over, an' fittit it on my feùt, t' wife clap't her hands an' shootit, 'I can dee't, Tom! I can dee't! an' thoo sall hev a par of *white* spats. There's nowte maks a man leùk sa like a gentleman as clean white spats! Did t'e iver see Dr. Dick Ringer o' Cockermouth? Well, what was't 'at meàd him ola's leùk cleaner, an' breeter, an' fresher, an' better-like nor anybody theear? Whey, nowte at o' else but t' white spats 'at he used to weear ivery day! I'll mak thee a par o' spats oot o' pooar oald uncle Geordie's corduroys 'at wadn't gang on the', an' I'll mak them i' time for the' to put on when thoo gangs to Peerith nixt market day!' I so' it was nea use sayin' she sudn't, if I'd been that way inclined, an' I wasn't; sooa she set to wark off hand, an' ripp't doon t' white breeks, an' pin't Charley's pattren on t' cleàth, an' cot it up by 't; an', as her heart was set on t' job, she hed t' spats finish't lang afoor t' time she said. When we com to try them on, yan on them was a varra decent fit, but t' tudder wasn't: it seem't to stand off whoar it sud sit clwose, an' to sit clwose whoar it sudn't; an' it was a gay while afooar we fund oot t' reason on't. But I happn't, at last, to glime up at hūr, an' ther was mair trūbble iv her feàce ner I'd iver seen afooar. 'Bliss thy heart, Mary!' says I, 'whativer's t' matter wid the'? Thoo leuks as if thy poddish was welsh?' 'Doesn't thoo see?' she says. 'Can tè nūt see 'at I've meàd them beàth for t' seàm feùt? Whoar's thy eyes, thoo mafflin?' says she, tackin' it oot o' me acoase she was mad at hersel', 'Whoar's t' een on the', I wūnder, 'at thoo doesn't see t' buttons is at t' inside o' t' ya feùt, an' t' ootside o' t' tudder?' 'By jing,' says I, 'an' seea they urr! Thoo *hes* meàd a fist on't! Thoo *hes* tailior't till a bonnie end! If this be thy tailiorin', I think thoo'd better stick till thy hoose-keepin' wark for t' rist o' thy life!' But I so' t' watter gedderin' iv her eyes, an' I so' 'at it no'but wantit anudder wūrd or two to mak' her blurt reet oot, an' seea I said nea mair. O' at yance she breeten't up ageàn, an' pot her arm roond my neck an' ga'e me a kiss, an' said, 'Niver fret aboot it, Tom lad,' says she, 'ther's aneùf left o' t' oald britches to mak anudder par o' spats. Thoo's gitten two for t' reet feùt, an' thoo sall hev two for t' left, an' than thoo need niver gang frae heàm adoot white spats to thy feet, for t' ya par 'ill wesh t' tudder, thoo sees!'

"I thowte I *was* gā'n to be set up wi' spats for sure, for she went at t' oald corduroy ageàn feùrcer nor iver, an' hed two mair meàd afoor I ken't whoar I was. She hed them o' wesh't an' iron't, an' straps putten on them, ruddy for gā'n to chūrch o' t' Sunday

Tom Railton's White Spats. 153

mwornin'; but loavin' bliss us o' weel! if she hedn't geàn an' meàd o' t' fower for t' reet feùt, an' left me just as far off hevin' spats to my feet as iver. Mad as we war, we beàth brast oot laùghin', an' laugh't tull hūr laugh hed rayder less of a cry in't nor it hed at t' fūrst, an' than says I, 'What's to be deùn noo, Mally!' I says, 'Urr we to send till Ireby for anudder par o' t' drip white corduroys, an' hev fower par o' spats? I is gā'n to be weel spattit i' t' lang run!' 'Nay,' says she, 'I'll spat the' na mair spats; I'll lig thur i' my oan top-dro'er, an' wheniver I see them they'll be a warnin' to me nūt to mell wi' wark 'at I hevn't been browte up till. Fwoke says it taks nine tailiors to mak' a man, but I divn't think anybody hes tell't us hoo many women it may tak' to mak' a tailior; but whedder it tak's many or few, thoo may mak' thysel' seàf an' suer 'at thy wife willn't be yan o' them.' An' that was t' way I was deùn oot o' my chance o' gittin' two par o' spats."

A SNECK POSSET.

IVER ageàn, Eddy! Niver ageàn!
    If I moo'n't hev a lad 'at 'ill coort me my
        leàn,
'At 'ill hod by ya sweetheart, an' me be that yan,
    I mūn bide as I is till I dee.
Thū's coddel't Keàt Crosstet, Ann Atchin, Jane
    Blair,
'Becca Rudd, Mary Mo'son, Ruth Lytle, an' mair;
Thoo says it's o' fūn, an' sec fūn ma' be fair,
    But it doesn't seem jannic to me.

I favour't the', ey! abeùn o' t' lads aboot;
I thowte, like a feùl, 'at thū'd sing-elt me oot
Frae t' tūdders, an' I've been reet sarra't, na doobt,
    To trust sec a taistrel as thee.
Reet sarra't? Ey, mess! I was warn't gaily weel,—
I was tel't hoo thū'd feùl't an' than left Greàcy Peile;
An' what reet hed I to believe thoo wad deal
    Ayder fairer or fonter wi' me?

A Sneck Posset. 155

Fwoke tel't mé thoo com of a slape, sneeky breed;—
'At a tungue sec as thine seldom hung iv a heid;—
'At twice i' three times when thoo said owte, thoo leed;
    But I fanciet that hardly cūd be.
For 'Speàtry, I kent, was a hard-spocken pleàce,
An' I thowte 'at, may-hap, thū'd been wrang't aboot
    Greàce;—
God help mé!—I thowte I read t' truth i' thy feàce,
    When thoo swore thoo cared only for me.

We're silly, us lasses—We're maizlins, I know!
We're t' meàst teàn wi' them 'at oor frinds meàst
    misco';
An' when we're teàn in, we've to shear what we sow,
    An' to rue sec mistaks till we dee.
But leet com' i' time, an' it o' com' at yance,
I so't fair aneùf, but, to give thee ya chance,
I went by mysel' to Jane Loncaster's dance,
    Just to see if thoo dūd care for me.

Theear, hoaf oot o' seet, a bye corner I teùk,
An' thoo dūdn't cū' nār; nūt a smile nor a leùk
Dūd té kest to poor me, as I dark't i' my neùk,
    An' wūnder't I'd trustit i' thee.
Thoo stack till Bess Bruff like a cockelty būr;
An' she cūtter't wi' thee jūst to greg Harry Scūrr;—
When t' cūshi'n com' in thoo teùk t' cūshi'n tull hur,
    An' thoo glimed, when thoo kiss't her, at me.

But Harry an' Bess meàd it up iv a crack;
An' noo, 'at thū's hed a begonk, thoo cū's back;
But if *thū's* fūnd oot *thine*, I've fūnd oot *my* mistak',
    An', I'll ho'd mysel' heart-heàl an' free.
Sooa Neddy, gud lad, dro' thy steàk, an' be gā'n;
Amang thy oald chances thū's m'appen finnd yan
Ma' be fain, though thū's snaip't her, to hev the' ageàn,
    But, Eddy! that yan isn't me.

REMARKS ON THE CUMBERLAND DIALECT.

The dialect of Cumberland, spoken in its purity only in the central parts of the county, may be admitted to be deficient in euphony; and, remarkable as it is for force and expression, its harshness of cadence renders it scarcely available for any poetry except the humorous or descriptive. By those unaccustomed or unattached to it, it may probably be considered hard and coarse even in prose compositions.

Its principal peculiarity is to be found in its vowel and dipthongal sounds, which, for the most part, are made either broader or deeper than in ordinary pronunciation; and this may be indicated with sufficient ease and distinctness, by means of phonetic spelling, when written or printed, to enable any reader, with a little practice and care, to pronounce broad Cumbrian with tolerable correctness.

The most important instances of this vowel peculiarity exist in the pronunciation of the long A and the short U, the former of which is sounded generally *yah* and the latter *uh;* thus to secure the Cumbrian pronunciation—ale must be spelled *yahl*, and ace *yahss*, lame is made *lyahm*, name *nyahm*, etc., etc., all monosyllabic, or, to prevent the accent being laid upon the Y, and so making two syllables, these words might be written *leahm*, *neahm*. As regards the U, the first syllable of cunning is in Cumberland lengthened out exactly to the sound of the German *kuhn*, and come is made *kuhm*. These sounds can only be conveyed by the interposition of the H.

When I first scribbled in the folk-speech of Cumberland I wrote it after this fashion, and the efficacy of the method was proved by the fact that intelligent or painstaking readers, knowing nothing of the dialect as spoken, were able to repeat the verses called "Branthet Neuk Boggle" in a style that might have satisfied even an exigeant professor of our Cumbrian philology.

The Cumberland dialect so written, however, had a remarkably ugly and uncouth appearance when printed, and the remonstrances of my present provincial publisher induced me to abandon the H orthography, and endeavour to secure the proper pronunciations by means of accent marks, spelling the words instanced above *leàm*, *neàm*, *cünning*, *cüm*, et similia similiter.

The broad O and Oa are in our Cumberland speech altered into *eà*, with the sound of *yah*, home becoming *heàm*, broad *breàd*, etc. There are exceptions to this as to most other rules, for lane is rendered as *lwoan* or *lonnin'*, choke as *chowk*, croak as *crowk*, road at *rwoad*, and more as *mair*, while shore has its ordinary sound. Almost in reversal of these changes, the broad A as in ball, a dance, Al, as in walk, Aw, as in awful, are sounded like the broad O or Oa, thus *boall*, *woak*, *oaful*, etc.; but the L is preserved in *oala's*, for always, scalp is pronounced *scowpe*, and ball, a plaything, is *bo'*, all, *oa'*, call, *co'*. hall, *ho'*, etc., etc.

Ea gets the pronunciation properly given to it in veal and mead; so that bread is *breed*, head, *heed*, dead, *deed*, etc., etc.; but when this dipthong precedes R, as in bear, wear, etc., it becomes dissyllabic like fear, as commonly pronounced, and mare too becomes *mee-ar*.

Ei becomes *ay*, either and neither becoming *ayder* and *nayder*, sometimes *owder* and *nowder*.

The broad I in bite, write, etc., the Cumbrians deepen almost as is done by well educated people in the southern counties, with notable exceptions however, the first personal pronoun being made Ah ; Igh, shortened and gutturalized by the Scotch, being sounded like *Ee*, night being *neet*, light, *leet*, etc., and find and bind pronounced like wind, viz.— *finnd, binnd*.

The double O is generally pronounced *eù*, or more exactly *yuh* shortly, fool being *feùl*, school, *'scheùl*, etc., in one short syllable. Do and too are often pronounced according to this rule, but almost equally often are made into *dee* and *tee*, while the preposition to is for the most part changed into *till* or *tull*.

With Ou and Ow Cumberland speakers are somewhat capricious, round being made *roond*, town, *toon*, etc., but found and bound become *fūnd* and *būnd*, ought, *owte*, nought, *nowte*, etc.

O with the sound of the short U is treated in a very arbitrary manner—one being called *yan*, none, *nin*, and oven, *yubben*.

Qu is generally softened into *wh*, aspirated distinctly— quick being pronounced *whick*, and quite, *white*, and Quaker, with old people, is *Whaker*.

Y is sometimes converted into G, as in *garth* for yard, *garn* for yarn ; and again that habit is sometimes reversed, as in *yatt* for gate.

The corruptions or variations of consonants are not so marked as those of vowels. The most notable are the hardening of Th into Dd, making father, *fadder*, mother, *mūdder*, etc. ; and the dropping of the two last of the three letters in the definite article, well illustrated by the Whitehaven boy's reply to an enquiry as to what ships had come in :—"*T*' 'Enry, an' *t*' 'Ebe, an' *t*' Ant, an' *t*' Atlas, an' *t*' Aurora ;" i.e. the Henry, the Hebe, the Ant, the Atlas, and the Aurora. Then we may notice the discarding of the final letter from all words ending in ing, and changing that syllable in all present participles to *an*, the participle of pass being in Cumberland more like the French pass*ant* than the English pass*ing*; also the final age being made *ish*, as in *cabbish* for cabbage, *manish* for manage, etc. ; the final ous too undergoing the same change, as in *faymus* for famous, *parlish* for parlous, etc. ; also idge as in *poddish* for porridge, or primarily, potage.

V is often converted into B or Bb—evening, eleven, Whitehaven, being called *ebenin'*, *elebben*, *Whitehebben*, etc.

These corruptions and deviations comprise nearly all the points wherein the dialect of Cumberland differs in sound and pronunciation from ordinary English speech; and set forth roughly, as they are, (abbreviations explaining themselves, and archaic words being given in a concise glossary,) they may, with a little attention, enable the uninitiated reader to understand all the Cumbrian pieces contained in this volume.

Some irregular verbs, as well as some not commonly classed as irregular, are curiously varied in Cumbrian conjugations. I give a few of these, written down as they rise in recollection, and arranged Lindley Murray's fashion.

Present.	*Past.*	*Past Participle.*
Break	Brack	Brocken
Bring	Brong, and Brang	Browte
Brust (burst)	Brast	Brossen
Cleed (clothe)	Cleàd	Cled
Clim'	Clam	Clim't and Clum
Cūm (come)	Com	Cum't
Cut	Cot and Cuttit	Cutten
Drink	Drunk	Drucken & Drocken
Drive	Dreàv	Druvven
Fling	Flang	Flung
Git (get)	Gat	Gitten
Gi'e (give)	Gev	Gi'en
Ga and Gang (go)	Went	Geàn
Greet (weep)	Grat	Grūtten
Hit	Hat and Hot	Hitten
Ho'd (hold)	Hodit	Hodden
Let	Let	Letten

Present.	Past.	Past Participle.
Kest (cast)	Kest	Kessen
Knead	Knod	Knodden
May	May'd or Med	
Mun (must)	Mūd	
Put	Pot	Putten
Rive	Reàv	Ruvven
Run	Ron	Run
Rise	Reùz	'Ruzzen
Stick	Stack	Stuck and Stucken
Set	Set	Setten
Tak	Tok and Teùk	Tocken
Thrust	Thrustit	Throssen

Minced or modified oaths are remarkably numerous in Cumberland, and in very common use. Most of them have descended from the old Roman Catholic times when, as Dr. Newman in speaking of Roman Catholic populations of the present day, avers, habitual swearing indicated piety and reverence for things sacred, and not profaneness. As heard now in Cumberland, these ancient expletives are as void of piety as of profanity, being used without any knowledge of their original signification, and merely to add force to asseveration, and to express, as varied in tone, surprise, disgust, pleasure, or indeed almost any feeling or emotion whatever. I append a few of these with their probable, often obvious, etyma :—

'Scush or Skerse	God's curse
Goy, and Goy Sonn	God, and God's Son
Gock, and Gock Sonn	Ibid. Ibid.
'Od's wuns an' deeth	God's wounds and death
Loavin' days	Loving Jesus
'Od's wintry wuns	God's sundry, or wondrous, wounds
'Od's wyte leet on thee	God's blame fall on you

'Od rot, 'Od sink, etc., etc.	See *Dickinson's* Glossary
' Marry	By Mary
' Mess	By the Mass
Där, Dy, and Dyne	Damn
Faix, and Faikins	Faith
Cock's wunters	God's wonders
Loze	Lord
My song	My soul
Deil bin	Devil be in

The peculiarities of the Scottish dialect have been explained by many writers, much more ably, as well as more at length, than may be done by me. Therefore the only assistance towards the understanding my Scots rhymes that I offer the reader is to intermingle, in the glossary appended, such Scottish words as I have used, with those proper to Cumberland and those common to both sides the Border.

The brief glossary here given consists, then, only of the words used in Scotland or Cumberland, or both, which appear in the foregoing *Tales and Rhymes;* corruptions and abbreviations being omitted. The significations I alone am answerable for, having, in nearly all instances, adopted the sense I can recollect the words being used in by the people speaking them in their daily talk. The quotations are intended to make these significations more intelligible, and also, by showing the manner in which the words so illustrated are used by others, to prove that the meanings I have so adopted are generally correct.

A GLOSSARY

OF

SCOTCH AND CUMBRIAN WORDS

OCCURRING IN THE RHYMES AND TALES
CONTAINED IN THIS VOLUME.

C signifies that the word it follows is Cumbrian. S that it is Scotch. S and C that it is common to both dialects.

A.

Addle, or Eddle, C, earn.

"What, I mun tak' my flale wimma, antres I git a job er two a threyshin, Ise *addle* summat be't."
Rev. T. Clarke. Johnnie Shippard.

Aiblins, S, perhaps.

" But *aiblins* neighbour ye have not the heart,
An' downa eithly wi' the cunzie part."
Ramsay. The Gentle Shepherd.

Aneuf, C, enough in quantity.

Anew, C, enough in number.

"We've *anew* o' sec as thee, an' *aneuf* o' what thou brings wid thee."—Said to a Hawker.

Aslew, C, amiss, out of course.

"There's nowte sa far *aslew* but gud manishment med set it streight."—Proverb.

Atweel, S, I wot well. Used to strengthen either affirmation or denial.

"Are they a' Johnie's?
Eh! *atweel* na;
Twa o' them were born
When Johnie was awa."
      Song—We're a' Noddin'.

B.

Back-end, C, late autumn.
"T' *back-end's* ola's t' bare-end."—Proverb.

Bain, C, near, convenient. Used in most of the northern counties.
"I swin'd my ways t' *bainest* geeat ower t' fell into Sleddle."
    Rev. T. Clarke. Johnnie Shippard.

Bairn, S, a child; Barne, C.
"Maidens' *bairns* are aye weel bred."—Proverb.
"They hed *barnes* an' bits o' flesh persirv'd i' bottles as fwok does berries."—*Ritson*. The Borrowdale Letter.

Barken't, S and C, encrusted.
"For God-seak put that barne in t' dolly-tūb an' scrūb't: it's fairly *barken't* ower wid mūck."—Said of a rarely washed infant.

Barrow-back't, C, bent by heavy work, such as wheeling loaded *barrows*.
"He's gitten bow't an' *barrow-back't*, an' wizzent sair o' t' feàce."—Heard at Ullock.

Batt, S and C, a blow.
"At ya *batt* he fell't me flat,
'Od dye! he'll be a darter."
    Mark Lonsdale. The Upshot.

Baul', S, bold, fierce.
"The first fuff o' a fat haggis is aye the *baul'est*."—Proverb.

Beàdless, C. This adjective is used to signify intolerable in suffering, and also impatient of pain—thus
"He says t' pain's *beàdless*, but than he's a *beàdless* body."
      Said to a Doctor.

Beck, C, a rivulet.
"Change is leetsome, if it's no'but oot o' bed intil t' *beck*."
Proverb.

Beel, C, to bellow like a bull.
"Summet tha caw't roworgins began a *beelin'* like a hundred mad bulls, an' as many lal lads i' ther sarks began a screamin' murder, I think, for ivery *beel* was like thunner."
Ritson. The Borrowdale Letter.

Begonk, Old S and C, a disappointment, "a sell."
"Now Cromwell's gane to Nick; an' ane ca'd Monk
Has played the Rumple a richt slee *begunk*."
Ramsay. The Gentle Shepherd.

Begood, S, began.
"The baronne he *begood* to bob,
No longer colde he stande."
Hogg. Lyttil Pynkie.

Beild, S and C, shelter.
"Better a wee buss than nae *beild*."
Proverb. *Burns's* Motto.

"Weal *beealt* frae t' fell wind by some heeh crags."
Rev. T. Clarke. T' Reysh-bearin'.

Bein, S, snug, comfortable.
"Were your *bein* rooms as thinly stocked as mine,
Less ye wad lose, and less wad ye repine."
Ramsay. The Gentle Shepherd.

Belyve, S and C, by and bye.
"*Belyve* the elder bairns come drapping in."
Burns. Cotter's Saturday Night.

Ben, S, the inner part of a house.
"It's ill bringing but what's no *ben*."—Proverb.

Bent, S, a coarse hard grass; applied also to the sterile land where bent grows.
"Gin ye'll consent to scour the *bent*
Wi' me, a rantin' Hielandman."
Hamilton. Song.

Billie, S, brother.
> "Be of gude cheir, now, Archie lad!
> Be of gude cheir, now, dear *billie*."
>
> Ballad—Archie o' Ca'field.

Bink, S, a bench for sitting upon.
> "For faut o' wise fouk feuls sit on *binks*."—Proverb.

Birl, S, to drink in conviviality; also to spend money in drinking.
> "When they were at the supper set
> An' *birlin'* at the wine."
>
> Ballad—Young Huntin.

> "She took me in, she set me doon,
> An hecht to keep me lawin' free;
> But, cunning carlin' that she was,
> She gar't me *birl* my bawbee."
>
> Song—Andro' wi' his cutty gun.

In the lake country the attendants who serve the drink round at sheep-shearings, etc., are called *burlers*.

Birkie, S, a brisk forward fellow.
> "See yon *birkie* ca'd a lord."
>
> *Burns.* For a' that.

Black-kites, C, bramble berries; in some parts called brummel-kites, in others black-bums.
> "I wantit grog—she brong mē *black-kite* wine."
>
> Heard at Harrington.

Blate, S and C, bashful.
> "A *blate* cat maks a proud mouse."—Proverb.

> "I've wonder't oft o' leàte
> What made thee leùk sea skar an' seem sea *bleàte*."
>
> *Graham.* Gwordie and Will.

Bleeze, S and C, flame.
> "In winter when he toils through wind and rain,
> A *bleezin'* ingle and a clean hearth-stane."
>
> *Ramsay.* The Gentle Shepherd.

Blether, S and C, noisy silly talk, loquacity.
>" A lawyer neist, wi' *bletherin'* gab,
> Wha speeches wove like onie wab."
>> Old Song—Jenny's Bawbee.

>" Chaps like these, like butterflees,
> Win owte wi' pride an' *blether*."
>> *Anderson.* Laird Johnie.

Blink, S, glance.
>" The evening sun was ne'er sae sweet
> As was the *blink* o' Phemie's e'e."
>> *Burns.* Blythe was she.

Blurt, C; Blirt, S, sudden burst of weeping, etc.
>"The lassie lost her silken snood,
> Whilk cost her monie a *blirt* an' bleer e'e."
>> Song.

Blythe, S, cheerful, happy.
>" A *blythe* heart mak's a blooming look."—Proverb.

Bood, S, behoved to.
>" Weel leese me o' you, Souter Jock,
> For tricks ye *bood* be tryin'."
>> *Ferguson.* The Election.

Boune, Old S, to journey or go.
>" Win up ! win up, now, Hynde Etin,
> Win up, an' *boune* wi' me."
>> Ballad—Hynde Etin.

Bowk, S and C, to retch.
>" For aye ye sup the brose at e'en
> Ye *bowk* at in the morn, lassie."
>> Song—Ye ha'e lain wrang, lassie.

Brae, S, bank of a stream, brow.
>"'Neath the *brae* the burnie jooks."
>> *Tannahill.* Gloomy Winter.

Brackin', C; Breckan, S, the common fern *(Pteris Aquilina)*.

A lady near Hawkshead having bought a small fern plant at a flower show, a neighbour exclaimed, "Three and sixpence for a lile *brackin !* I'd ha' browte her a leeàd o' them for't !"

>" Round the sylvan fairy nooks
> Feathery *breckans* fringe the rocks."
>> *Tannahill.* Gloomy Winter.

Brant, C, steep.
>"Old Man! Old Man! your sides are *brant.*"
>>The Old Man.

Brat, S and C, apron; (used frequently for clothing in general.)
>"To get them *brats*, then, ye maun toil an' spin."
>>*Ramsay.* The Gentle Shepherd.

"To see her whol'd stockings, her *brat*, an' her gown."
>>*Anderson.* Our Sukey.

Braw, S, fine, handsomely attired.
>"Upon the banks o' flowing Clyde
>The lasses busk them *braw.*"
>>*Burns.* Of a' the Airts.

Break, C, a joke, a bit of fun.
>"Joe Tyson teem't a pint o' yall doon Danny Towson' back. Wasn't that a *break?*"—Heard at Dean.

Buirdly, S, stout, strongly made.
>"They say ill ale has been the deid
>O' monie a *buirdly* loon."
>>*Ferguson.* Leith Races.

Burn, S, a brook.
>"Beside that brig, out owre that *burn*,
>Where water bickereth bright and sheen."
>>Ballad—Thomas the Rhymer.

Burnewin, S, a blacksmith (burn the wind).
>"An' *burnewin* comes on like death
>At every chaup."
>>*Burns.* Scotch Drink.

But, S, the outer apartment of a house.
>"The auld wife cried *but* the house, 'Jenny, come ben.'"
>>Song—The Yellow Hair'd Laddie.

But, S, without (probably from *be out*).
>"Beauty but bounty's but bauch."—Proverb.

But and, Old S, also, likewise.
>"Adieu, madame, my mother dear,
>*But and* my sisters three."
>>Ballad—Lord Maxwell's Good Night.

Byspel, C, a mischevious person.
"It's a fair *byspel* 'at is't. It breaks o' 'at cūms iv it 'geàt."

C.

Cabbish-skrunt, C; Kail-runt, S, the stalk of a cabbage.
"*Cabbish-skrunt* pultess is grand for biles."
        Said by a rustic Doctor.

Canny, C, (Connie in Furness, etc.) nicé, attractive, pleasant.
  "God speed ye weel! a *cannier* pair
  Ne'er kneeled afore a priest."
     Miss Blamire. The Sailor Lad.

Canny, S, gentle, careful.
 "Be *cannie* wi' the cream."—A common legend on tea-ware.

Canty, S, happy, cheerful.
  "*Canty* war we ower yere kail,
  Toddy jugs an' draps o' ale."
    Hogg. The Laird o' Lamington.

Carle, S, a vulgar man.
"Auld gudeman ye're a drucken *carle*, a drucken *carle*."
     Sir A. Boswell. Song.

Carlin, S, a coarse old woman; feminine of Carle.
 On being told that the wives of the Scottish Judges claimed the title of "My Lady," their husbands being "My Lord," King James V. exclaimed, "I made the carles lords, but wha the deil made the *carlins* leddies?"

Chafts, S and C, the jaws.
  "On Seaton crafts they buff't their *chafts*,
  An' garrt them rin like daft, man."
     Skirvin. Tranent Muir.

  "At time when nowte but teeth was gawn,
  An' aw by th' *chafts* was tether't."
    Mark Lonsdale. The Upshot.

Chap, S, rap, strike or stroke.
  "An' quhan he cam' to Barnard's Ha'
  Would neither *chap* nor ca'."
     Ballad—Gilmorice.

Chiel', S, a man; generally applied to young men.

  "Weel we lo'e the *chiel'* we think
   Can get us tick or gi'e us drink."
        Ferguson. My Aul' Breeks.

Clash, C and S, scandal, gossip.

  "The king, the laws, the reets o' man,
   The parish *clash*, the empire's ban."
        Stagg. New Year's Epistle.

Clatter, S and C, superfluous, rapid or noisy talk.

"He that talks till himsel' *clatters* till a feul."—Proverb.

Clink, C, a sounding blow.

  "An' brong fisher Jemmy a *clink* i' the lug."
        Anderson. Burgh Reaces.

Clippin', C, sheep-shearing. A great festival on the larger dale farms. For a description see "The Old Man," first edition.

Clemm'd, C, starved with hunger. A Lancashire and Cheshire word.

Nixon, the Cheshire prophet, said he was "going to London to be *clemm'd*," and was accidentally shut up in a closet without food, and there found dead—so fulfilling his prophecy.

Clot-heed, C, blockhead.

"I is gà'n to be a *clot-heed*—I's leavin' nin for mysel'!"
  Anthony Gasgarth, carving a goose at a hunt dinner.

Clowk, C, clutch or grasp greedily.

"He meàd a *clowk* at my neckcloth and missed it."
        Said after a fight.

Cobbles, C, stones rounded by water-wear.

  "Smith Lytle fell oot wi' the *cobbles*,
   An' peel'd o' the bark off his shins."
        Anderson. The Codbeck Wedding.

Coddle, C, Cuddle, S, embrace.

  "I trimlin' steud an' dursn't speak,
   But fain wad *coddled* Peggy Penn."
        Anderson. Peggy Pen.

  "I've seen the day ye butter't my brose,
   An' *cuddlet* me late an' early."
  Old Song—The Deuks dang owre wi' my Daidie.

Corbie, S, the carrion crow.
"It's kittle shootin' at *corbies* or clergy."—Proverb.
Crack, S and C, converse ; also boast.
"They *crack't* away like bourtree guns."
Mark Lonsdale. The Upshot.
"Keep oot o' his company that *cracks* o' his cheatrie."
Proverb.
Croodle, or Cruddle, S and C, crouch or shrink.
" My bonnie wee *croodlin'* doo."
Old Song.
" We sat doon an' grat under a hedge or a wo', o' *cruddled* togidder."—*Betty Yewdale.* T' terrible Knitters i' Dent.
Crouse, S, brisk, bold, "bumptious."
"A cock's aye *crouse* on its ain midden-heed."—Proverb.
Cushion dance, C, the finishing dance at a rural ball or merry-night.

A young man, carrying a cushion, paces round the room in time to the appropriate tune, selects a girl, lays the cushion at her feet, and both kneel upon it and kiss, the fiddler making an extraordinary squeal during the operation. The girl then takes the cushion to another young man, who kisses her as before, and leaves her free to "link" with the first, and march round the room. This is repeated till the whole party is brought in, when they all form a circle, and "kiss out" in the same manner, sometimes varying it by the kissers sitting on two chairs, back to back, in the middle of the ring, and kissing over their shoulders—a trying process to bashful youth of either sex.

Cuttie, S, any thing short—as a spoon, pipe, etc.
" Better sup wi' a *cuttie* nor want a speun."—Proverb.
" Aul' Simon sat luntin' his *cuttie*,
An' lowsin' his buttons for bed."
Andrew Scott. Simon and Janet.

D.

Dadder, C, (Dodder in Furness, etc.) tremble, shiver.

I once heard a Cumberland youth, at a supper table, say, indicating a "shape" of jelly, " I'll tak sūm o' that *dadderin'* stuff."

Dadge, C, to plod along heavily.
"Then *dadged* we to the bog owre meedows dree,
To plet a sword and seevy cap for thee."
Relph. Cursty and Peggy.

Daft, S and C, foolish, silly.
"Glower't at me as he'd been *daft.*"
Song—The carl cam ower the craft.
"Ses I, 'A was niver larn't see *daftness.*'"
Rev. T. Clarke. Johnny Shippard.

Daized, C, stupified, benumbed.
"Theer war we stannin', dodderin' an' *daiz't* wi' cauld, as neer deead as macks nea matter."
Betty Yewdale. T' terrible Knitters i' Dent.

Dark, C, to lurk, keep unseen,
"On her leànly bed she toss'd her,
Darkin' till the tempest ceas'd."
Stagg. The Return.

Darrak, C, day's-work.
"An' as for a *darrak* in barn or in meedow,
Whee match'd me when just i' my prime."
Anderson. Twee auld Men.

Dicht, S, wipe, or cleanse.
"An' aye she *dichtit* her father's bluidy wounds,
When the blude ran reid as wine."
Ballad—The Douglas Tragedy.

Doff, C, (do off, old English) undress, strip.
"The bridesmaids o' wi' fusslin care
The bride, hauf-yieldin', *doff't.*"
Stagg. The Bridewain.

Don, C, (do on, old English) to dress.
"And up he rose, and he *donn'd* on his clothes,
And he d'upp'd the chamber door."
Hamlet.
"He's nicer in his war-day duds
Nor udders *don't* i' aw their best."
Anderson. Geordie Gill.

Donk, C, damp.
"It *donks* an' dozzles an' does, but niver cūms iv any girt pell."—A Boatman, on the Ullswater weather.

Dool, S, sadness.
    "Lang may I weep in *dool* an' sorrow."
              Hamilton. The Braes o' Yarrow.

Douce, S and C, respectable, well-behaved,
    "An' now I'm grown sae cursed *douce,*
    I pray and ponder but the house."
              Burns.
"The *douce* dapper lanleady criet 'Eat, an' be welcome.'"
          Anderson. The Bleckell Murry-Neet.

Doucht, S, could; Dowe in the past tense.
    "They held the nose an' crook't the mou',
    An' *doucht* na bide the smell."
             Hogg. The Witch o' Fife.

Dour, S, hard, stern.
    "I'll set her up on yon crab-tree,
    It's sour an' *dour,* an' so is she."
               Old Rhyme.

Dow, S, can, is able.
"Gin we canna do as we wad, we maun do as we *dowe.*"
              Proverb.

Dowly, C, melancholy, dismal.
"When we turn't round Windermere Watter heead, t' waves blash't seea *dowly* 'at we war fairly heart-brossen."
      Betty Yewdale. T' terrible Knitters i' Dent.

Dree, S, suffer; C, slow, lingering, also to move slowly.
"*Dree* out the inch when ye've tholed the span."—Proverb.
    "Six *dree* year hed Susan languish'd
    Sen her Walter went away."
           Stagg. The Return.

Drook, S, drench.
    "An' aye she took the tither sook
    To *drook* the stoury tow."
         Song—The weary pun' o' tow.

Drouthy, S, thirsty.
> "The well o' life is dribbling dry,
>   An' *drouthy, drouthy's* kimmer an' I."
>   Song—My Kimmer and I.

E.

Eerie, S, fearful, or calculated to cause superstitious fear or awe.
> "Gloomy, gloomy was the nicht,
>   An' *eerie* was the way."
>   Old Ballad—Young Tamlane.

Egg, or Egg on, C, incite, urge.
> "He was a rare *egg*-battle."—*Dickinson.* Lamplugh Club.

Eldritch, S, unearthly.
> "Quhan words he found, their *eldritch* sound
>   Was like the norlan' blast."
>   *Dr. Jamieson.* The Water Kelpie.

F.

Fash, S and C, trouble, annoy, bother (noun and verb).
> "Ye're sair *fashed* haudin' naething together."—Proverb.
> "Oald clish ma clash, thou's nowt but *fash*—
>   Ga heam to bed, 'Od dye thee!"
>   *Mark Lonsdale.* The Upshot.

Feal, S, comfortable.
> "Frae tap to tae that cleeds me weel,
>   An' haps me *feal* an' warm at e'en."
>   *Burns.* My Spinning Wheel.

Feck, S, a considerable quantity or number, most part.
> "Wae sucks for him that has nae *feck* o' 't."
>   *Ferguson.* Gude Braid Claith.

Feckless, S and C, feeble, useless.
> "*Feckless* fowk are aye fain."—Proverb.
> "A thowte A sud no'but meeak a varra *feckless* fend, if A was witch'd seck a parlish lang way fray heeam."
>   *Rev. T. Clarke.* Johnny Shippard.

Fells, C, hills.

"If there were nea *fells* there wad be nea deals."—Proverb.

Few, C. This word is hardly translatable, but means to set about a task in a manner likely to accomplish it.

" I't' chimla neùk some gay gud han's,
  An' gaily ill to slocken,
  Set tea wi' porringers an' pans,
  An' *few't* weel to get drucken."
      Mark Lonsdale. The Upshot.

Fewsome, C, capable-looking, workman-like.

"She warm'd him up some keàl,
An' Ralph dud mak a varra *fewsome* meàl."
      Graham. Gwordie and Will.

Flaitch, C, Fleech, S, coax. Sometimes used as a noun, thus—

"He's a fair *flaitch* when he wants owte."—Said of me.

" She *fleech't* him fairly to his bed
  By ca'in' him her burdie."
      Christ's Kirk on the Green.

Flaucht, S, flash.

" Ae fire-*flaucht* darted through the rain,
  Where a' was dark afore."
      Kirkpatrick Sharp. Murder of Carlaverock.

Flay, C, Fley, S, to frighten.

"*Fleyin'* a bird 's no the gate to grip it."—Proverb.

This word has its substantive form in *flayan*—
A blue-devilled fellow at Coniston said he could not stay in his house because there was *flayan* in it. "Ey," said his mother, "If there isn't there will be—there 'ill be empty cupboards, ther needn't be wār *flayan* nor that!"

Fletherin, S, flattering.

"*Fletherin* fowk's maistly fause fowk."—Proverb.

Flipe, C, a hat rim.

A retired sea-captain at Whitehaven used to be called "*Flipy* Fisher," on account of his broad brim.

Flyte, S and C, scold.
> "An' gin she tak' the thing amiss,
> E'en let her flyte her fill, Jo."
> Song—Steer her up.

Font, C, fond, foolishly attached, "spooney."
> "Whey, Gworge, thou's owder feul or *font*,
> To think o' sec a frow."
> *Anderson.* Betty Brown.

Foorsett, C, to get in front of and face, to intercept.

A ghost used to haunt the "Crossgates" in Lamplugh, of which it was said, "Whativer way folk turns it *foorsetts* them."

Footh and Foothy, S and C, abundance, well provided, plentifully stocked.
> "He's brought *footh* o' foreign trash,
> An' dibbled it in our yairdie."
> Song—The wee wee German Lairdie.

"It's a *foothy* hoose is Betty Turnbull's."
> Said by old Cuddy Wilson at Workington.

Foregather, S, meet.
> "To bear the milk-bowie nae pain was to me,
> When I at the buchtin' *foregathered* wi' thee."
> *Ramsay.* The Gentle Shepherd.

Forfouchten, S, over fatigued, exhausted.
> "I'm but like a *forfouchten* hound
> Has been fechtin' in a dirty syke."
> Ballad—Hobbie Noble.

Fratch, C, quarrel.
> "He's just a *fratchin'*, feightin' feul."
> *Anderson.* Dick Watters.

Fusionless, S, pithless, insipid.
> "God! the aul' doited body's as *fusionless* as a docken!"
> *Michael Scott.* Tom Cringle's Log.

G.

Ga, C; Gang, S and C, go.
> "I'll *gang* nae mair to yon toon."
> *Burns.* Song.

Gangrel, S, vagrant.
> "A merry core
> O' randy *gangrel* bodies."
> > Burns. The Jolly Beggars.

Gar, S, make, compel.
> "The first Scots kirk that they cam' to
> They *garr't* the bells be rung;
> The next Scots kirk that they cam' to
> They *garr't* the mass be sung."
> > Ballad—The Gay Goss-hawk.

Gay, C; Gey, S, (adverb form, Gaily) tolerable, considerable.
"Here's a *gay* canny mwornin'."—A common salutation.
"No verra, but *gey*."—By-saying.
"Hoo irr ye preuvin?" "*Gaily, gaily,* gangin' aboot!"
> A common salutation and reply.

Geàl, C, split, rend, ache severely as from cold.
"I've an oald teuth, when t' coald gits tull't, it maks o' *geàl* ageàn."—Said to a Doctor.

Gear, S and C, wealth, substance.
> "A gleib o' lan'—a claut o' *gear*
> Was left me by my auntie, Tam."
> > Burns. Ane an' twenty, Tam.

> "Bruff-side lairds bang't aw the rest
> For braggin' o' their *gear*."
> > Anderson. Bleckell Murry-Neet.

Ged, S, the pike.
> "Now safe the stately saumon sail,
> An' trouts bedropp'd wi' crimson hail,
> An' eels weel kenn'd for souple tail,
> An' *geds* for greed."
> > Burns. Tam Samson.

Gezlin, C and S, goslin, young goose.
> "Peat' lass, wid her yallow muffs,
> Steud kaakin like a *gezlin*."
> > Mark Lonsdale. The Upshot.

"If I canna keep geese I'll keep *gezlins*."—Proverb.

12

Ghem, ga way tull't, C, game, go to it; a hunting phrase; used proverbially to signify any attractive fun or quarreling.

"There was a fine see howe—an' *ghem ga way tull't.*"

Gin, S, if.

"*Gin* a body meet a body."
            Song—Coming through the Rye.

Gledge, S, look slyly.

"Mr. Forret, alias *Gledgin* Gibbie, had borne the brunt of incensed kirk-sessions before that time.
            Hogg. Tibbie Hyslop.

Glent, S and C, gleam.

"Where flowers an' gowans wont to *glent*,
I' bonnie blinks beside the bent."
            Ferguson. Auld Reekie.

Gliff, C and S, glimpse.

"Here, here it was (a wae leet on the pleace)
'At furst I gat a *gliff* o' Betty's feace."
            Relph. Harvest.

Glime, C, look sideways.

"'Twad mak a deid man laugh to see
Them *glime* at yen anudder."
            Anderson. The Village Gang.

Gloamin', S, twilight.

"The *gloamin'* grey out owre the welkin keeks."
            Ferguson. The Farmer's Ingle.

Gloom, S, frown.

"Still away his heid was shyin',
Gloomin' like a boxing bull."
            John Johnston. Dear Meal Johnnie.

Glower, S and C, stare.

"He *glower't* at the mune till he fell i' the midden."
            Proverb.

"What's t'e *glowerin'* at? Does t'e see any cat' horns?"
            Sauce.

Glump, C, sulk.

"Neist time we met he *glump't* an' glower't
An' leukt anudder way."
            Anderson. The lass abeun thirty.

God speed, C, a small wooden partition or screen placed within the house door, when it opens directly upon the sitting room. It has probably been called so from departing guests being wished "God Speed" beside it. I first heard the word at Harrington, from a humourist who asked a group of neighbours if they'd seen Tommy Wilson, who lived next door to him, adding, "If ye sud see him, tell him 'at his barns an' mine hev been feightin' till they've knock'd t' *God-speed* doon." The fun of this lay in the well known fact that both were childless.

Gorb, C, an unfledged bird.

"Geàp, *gorbie*, an' thou'll git a würm."—Proverb.

Gowk, S and C, cuckoo, fool.

"Ye breed o' the *gowk*, ye've nae rhyme but ane."—Proverb.

"'Bout kings and councils *gowks* mak fratch."
     Anderson. Gud strang yell.

Gowl, C, to weep vociferously, to howl.

"It greàn't, an' it *gowl't*, an' it freetent fwoke sair."
    Dickinson. Scallow-Beck Boggle.

Gradely, C, a Lancashire and Cheshire word, often used in Cumberland, signifying proper or correct. I have overheard myself, in contravention of the proverb, spoken of as "a varra *gradely* man" in the lake district.

Grank, C, to covet querulously.

"Hout man ! what signifies repinin',
Or *grankin'*, snifterin', twistin', twinin'."
    Stagg. New Year's Epistle.

Greet, S and C, weep.

"It's nae mair to see a woman *greet* than to see a goose gang barefit."—Proverb.

"When we'd hed our belly full o' *greetin'* we gat up, an' feel't better for't."—*Betty Yewdale.* T' terrible Knitters i' Dent.

Greg, C, tantalize.

"It does *greg* yan to hear a hunt yan cannot see."
  Said by a veteran hunter whose sight was failing.

Gruesome, S, making the flesh creep with disgust or horror.

"An' though she wore a human face,
It was a *gruesome* sight to see."
    Hogg. The Spirit of the Glen.

Gud his-sel', C, felicitate, or gratify himself.

"Gi'e me anudder kiss." "Nay, thou mun *gud thysel'* wid what thou's gitten !—thou's git nea mair to-neet."
An over-heard conversation.

Guff, S and C, a silly fellow.

"When sec-like *guffs* leame decent fwoke,
It's time some laws sud alter."
Anderson. The Village Gang.

Gumption, C, tact, cleverness.

"Hed I thy *gumption* or thy gift o' gob."
Graham. Geordie and Will.

Gyversome, C, voracious, ravenous.

"T' mair ye give till greedy fwoke t' mair *gyversome* they growe."—Proverb.

H.

Hag, C, to cut with an axe.

"He was seun back, wid his axe ower his shooder, an' begon to *hag* his way through t' deurr."
Dickinson. Lamplugh Club.

Hag-worm, C, the viper.

"Theear was beears, an' lions, an' tigers . . . an' girt yedtheran *hag-werms*, fower or five yerds lang."
Rev. T. Clarke. Johnny Shippard.

Hake, C, a riotous festivity, tumult.

"They drank the yell up ivery drop,
Wid nowder *hake* nor quarrel."
Mark Lonsdale. The Upshot.

Ham-sam, C, mingled promiscuously.

"Five or six gat on to t' bed,
An' sat *ham-sam* togidder."
Mark Lonsdale. The Upshot.

Hank, S and C, skein of thread or yarn; also a loop.

"O though thy hair were *hanks* o' gowd,
An' thy lips were droppin' hinnie."
Song—The Waukrife Minnie.

"And when the worsted *hanks* she wound,
Her skill was further proved."
S. Bamford. My Wynder.

Hantle, S and C, a considerable number or quantity.

Part of the Rev. Walter Dunlop's congregation at Dumfries having joined the Baptists, he alluded to the circumstance in the pulpit, thus—"I thocht till ha'e gethered under my wings, as a hen gethereth her chickens, but a *hantle* o' ye ha'e turn't oot to be deuks, an' ta'en to the water."

" I've been a sad deevil, an' spent gowd i' gowpens,
But still I've a *hantle* left yet."
Anderson. Twee Auld Men.

Hap, S and C, cover.
" Ance as gude
As ever *happit* flesh an' blude."
Ferguson. My Aul' Breeks.

Haver, (pron. Havver) C, oats, oaten.
" Our Ellik likes fat bacon weel,
A *haver* bannock pleases Dick."
Anderson. Gud strang Yell.

Hay-bay, C, uproar.
" Wi' whiskey they weetit their wizzens,
An' seun a sad *hay-bay* began."
Anderson. The Clay Daubin'.

Heartsome, S and C, cheerful, pleasant.
" Let's creep ower the *heartsome* turf ingle,
An' laugh the wild winter away."
Anderson. The days that are gane.

Heeze, S, hoist, elevate.
" Thae bonnie bairn time Heaven has sent
Still higher may it *heeze* ye."
Burns. A Dream.

Heids an' thraws, S, lying in irregular positions in bed or elsewhere.

"Lie *heids an' thraws* like Jock an' his mither."—Proverb.

Herdwick, C, probably formed like bailiwick, etc., and first applied to the portion of hill-pasture assigned to the herds of each dale farm ; now used to distinguish the hardy, active breed of sheep grazed upon the *herdwicks*.

"He breaks bands like a *herdwick* tip" is a proverbial saying I have heard applied to a rustic scape-grace.

Herk, S, whisper.

"When a Scotchman wants you to listen he says 'speak,' and when he wants you to whisper he says '*herk.*'"—*Anon.*

Hirple, S and C, limp, walk lamely.

"The hares were *hirplin* doon the furs."
Burns. The Holy Fair.

"Jack Mar, the *hirplin* piper's son,
Can bang them o' at leein'."
Anderson. The Village Gang.

Hoaf-thick, C, half-wit, thick-head.

"Than Watty Ferguson, provwok't
To hear this *hoaf-thick* rattle."
Stagg. The Bridewain.

Hoddingly, C, persistently.

"Does your pain come and go?" "It nayder cūms ner ga's; it's theear *hoddingly.*"—Said to a Doctor.

Hooal't, or Whoal't, C, holed, "bagged," applied to anything being secured, thus—

At a school treat in High Furness I was "scrambling" comfits, and having filled a paper packet with gravel, and thrown it up, it was caught by a great hulking fellow, who thrust it into his pocket, exclaiming, "I've *hooal't* that an'." His face, when his attention was directed to the contents of his prize, was a sight.

Hosteler, Old S, keeper of an inn or hostel.

"Syne pay him on a gantree,
As *hosteler* wives should do."
Old Song—The Maltman.

Hork, S, to burrow.

"The mouse is a wee merrie beastie;
The mowdie *horks* wantin' the een."
Old Song—Brose and Butter.

Hound-trail or dog trail, C, a drag hunt.

"Whist's as much afooar lant (loo) as a fox-hunt's afooar a *dog-trail.*"—Heard at a Merry-Night.

How, S and C, hollow, empty.

"A house looks *how* without a wife."
Anderson. Tib and her Maister.

Howk, S and C, excavate.
> "She has *howkit* a hole baith deep and wide,
> She has putten them in baith side by side."
> Old Ballad—The Cruel Mother

How-strowe, C, in confusion.
> "Thy plew gear's liggin' *how-strowe,*
> An' somebody's stown thee thy cou'ter."
> *Mark Lonsdale.* Johnnie.

Hugger-mugger, C, huddled up, out of order or system.
> "Thus in *hugger-mugger* make a marriage."
> *Shakspeare.*

Most philologists hold that this word signifies private or surreptitious; but in Cumberland, where it is still in common use, the sense is as above.

Huller't, C, coagulated or clotted—applied to blood.

I have heard of an up and down fight in a public-house, where "T' *huller't* bleud laid an inch thick on t' flooer."

I

Ilka, or Ilk, S, each.
> "*Ilka* blade o' grass keps its ain drop o' dew."
> Proverb, and Song by *J. Ballantyne.*

Intak, C, a piece of land taken in from the common.
> "T' *intak's* t' best o' t' grund."—Said by a Dale-farmer.

Iverly, C, everly, continuously.
> "How often do you take your ale?" "Yall? I tak it *iverly!*" "*Iverly?*" "Ey, ebben endways away!"
> Part of a professional conversation.

J

Jannic, C, a Lancashire word, signifying fair or honest.
> "Thoo hes ower mickle jaw to be *jannic.*"
> Said to a voluble Auctioneer.

Jink, S, to escape suddenly, a rapid evasion.
> "Our billie's gi'en us a' the *jink,*
> An' owre the sea."
> *Burns.*

Job-jurnal, C, a toy on the principle of a humming top, but made with a shouldered stick passed through a perforated nut-shell and an apple, or failing that, a potato stuck upon the lower end, to be spun by pulling a string wrapped upon the shaft within the shell. In Furness this name is applied to the pig-nut, which in central Cumberland is called a *yowie-yorlin*, and in Dumfriesshire a *hornick*.

Joggle, C, to shake sharply, or violently.

"He dreàv us ower rwoads 'at varra nār *joggled* us to bits."
     Said by an old lady at Loweswater.

Jook, S, to shrink, or dip the head to elude observation or missile.

"It's past *jooking* when the heid's off."—Proverb.

K

Kail, S; Keàl, C, broth—so called from a frequent ingredient.

"He gat his *kail* in a riven dish."—Proverb.
  "Swoaps o' drink an' gud lythe *keàle*
   Cheer up each day."
    Stagg. The New Year's Epistle.

Kaim't, C, literally crooked, but used to signify cross, or peevish.

"Aa boddert my brain thinkan some on them ower,
An' than set to wark an' wreàtt doon three or fower
O't' *kaymtest* an' t' creuktest, like 'garrak' an' 'dyke-stower,'
Sek like as we use in oald Cummerlan'."
   Dickinson. The words of oald Cummerlan'.

Keàv, C, to dance awkwardly, throwing the legs clumsily about.

"That barn, says Hyne, i' Palmer' toft,
 'Ill dea reet weel to *keàv* in."
   Mark Lonsdale. The Upshot.

Keek, S and C, to peep.

"He that *keeks* through a keyhole may see what will vex him."—Proverb.
  "She conquers mair nor Bonnypart
   Whene'er she *keeks* aroun'."
    Anderson. The Thursby Witch.

Ken, S and C, know.
"*Ken* yersel and yere neighbours 'ill no mis-*ken* ye."
                                                Proverb.
Kirk-garth, C, church-yard.
"They tak meear pastime e what they see i' th' *kirk-garth* nor what they hear i' th' kirk."—*Mrs. Wheeler.* Dialogues.
Kit, C, a small tub or bucket.
"A riddlin'—a riddlin', an oald wife striddlin',
A *kit* full o' cunning things in a coald morning."
                                    An ancient conundrum.
Kimmer, S, a familiar designation for woman—something like gossip. The young women who assist at christenings are called "maiden *kimmers.*"
"How do ye, *kimmer?*
An' how do ye thrive—
An' how monie bairns ha'e ye?
Kimmer! I ha'e five."
                        Song—A' Noddin'.
Knowe, S, knoll, hillock.
"His gear may buy him glens an' *knowes.*"
                                    Burns. To Daunton me.

L.

Lafter, C, a brood of chickens, etc.; also a setting of eggs.
"I hevn't a ne'bour 'ill lend me a *lafter* of eggs."
                                    Said by a farmer's wife.
Laik, C, play.
"But *laiks* at wate-not-whats within
O' Sunday efterneun."
                        Relph. After Horace.
Laikins, C, playthings, toys.
"Here's babby-*laikins*—rowth o' spice,
On sto's an' stands extended."
                        Stagg. Rosley Fair.
Lait, C, seek.
"Lads, i' t' dark, meade rampin' wark
Or cloaks an' clogs were *laitit.*"
                        Mark Lonsdale. The Upshot.

Lal, C, (in the northern and southern parts, Lile) little.
>"I *lal* thowte fasts sec fearful things to bide."
>
>*Relph.* St. Agnes' Fast.

Lap, C, wrap.
>"*Lap't* my cranky neckcloth round his heid."
>
>*Graham.* Gwordie and Will.

Lave, S, the rest, remainder.
>"When a' the *lave* gang to their bed,
> I wander dowie up the glen."
>
>Song—Heelan' Harry.

Lawin, S, a public house reckoning.
>"Gude wife, count the *lawin*,
> An' bring a drappie mair."
>
>*Burns.* Song.

Leal, or Leil, S, true, pure, loyal.
>"O gi'e me a token o' love, sweet May—
> A *leil* love-token true."
>
>*A. Cunningham.* The Mermaid.

Leàne, your leàne, his leàne, etc., S and C, lone, solitary.
>"An' when, sweet lassie, you're ye're *leàne*,
> This heart o' mine wad joy to know."
>
>*Miss Blamire.* The Toiling Day.

Leàth, C, a barn.
>"Why ne had thou put the capel in the *lathe*."
>
>*Chaucer.* The Reeve's Tale.

Ley, C, a scythe.
>"Clogs, splinter new, bass-boddom'd chairs,
> An' *lea*-stanes for new *lea*ses."
>
>*Stagg.* Rosley Fair.

Lichtly, S, to make light of.
>"The lass that *lichtlies* may lament."—Proverb.

Lilt, S and C, a lively tune or song; or, as a verb, to sing merrily.
"Now haste ye turn King David ower,
An' *lilt* wi' holy clangour."
Burns.
It means also to rise on the toes in walking. Diomed's walk had a *lilt* in it as described by Ulysses, thus—
"I ken the manner of his gait,
He rises on the toe : that spirit of his
In aspiration lifts him from the earth."
Shakspeare. Troilus and Cressida.

Lippen, S, to trust.
"Ye'll deceive nane but them that *lippen* to ye."—Proverb.

Lirk, S and C, a wrinkle or fold.
"Sup sūm poddish, an' tak' t' *lirks* oot o' thy skin."
Said to a rustic convalescent.

Lish, C, active.
"When I was a *lish* laughing lass o' sixteen."
Anderson. Auld Robby Miller.

Loan, S ; Lonning, C, lane.
"The kye stood rowtin' in the *loan*."
Burns. The Twa Dogs.
"The lads an' the lasses i't' *lonning*
Wer' pairin' like sparrows i't' spring."
Anon. Raffles Merry-Neet.

Lock, C, a number or quantity.
"A gay *lock* o' fwoke hed gedder't up i' time to gang tillt' kurk, an' away they struttit."—*Dickinson.* Lamplugh Club.

Lofe, C, a chance of anything, an opportunity.
"Yance I hed t' *lofe* an' I'd luck to say no, an' I niver hed t' *lofe* ageàn."—Said by an elderly spinster.

Lonter, C, lounge, or loiter.
"*Lonterin'* fwoke's ola's lazy fwoke."—Proverb.

Loon, S, rogue.
"I tint my curch an' baith my shoon ;
Ah ! Duncan, ye're an unco *loon*."
Duncan Gray—Old Version.

Loot, S, stop.
> "He *lootit* doon her lips to kiss,
> O kiss foreboding woe."
> *C. K. Sharpe.* The Murder of Carlaverock.

Lowe, S and C, a flame.
> "To touch the glass her hand hes touch'd
> It sets them in a *lowe*."
> *Anderson.* The Thursby Witch.

Lown, or Lownd, S and C, calm, still.
> "Your chamber's very dark, fair maid,
> The nichte is wondrous *lown*."
> Ballad—Sir Roland.

Lowp, S and C, leap.
> "*Lowp* off the steed, says false Sir John,
> Yere bridal bed ye see."
> Ballad—May Colean.

> "My heart keeps such a rout,
> It *lowps* an' *lowps* as if it wad *lowp* out."
> *Ewan Clark.* Costard's Complaint.

Lowpy-back, C, leap-frog.
> "Ye've been laikin at *lowpy-back* o' t' rwoad heàm."
> Part of a scolding.

Lugs, S and C, ears.
> "I'll lay my *lugs* in Pindus' spring,
> And invocate Apollo."
> *Ramsay.*

> "Kursty, souple gammerstang,
> Ned Wilson brong his *lug* a whang."
> *Anderson.* The Worton Wedding.

Lum, S, chimney.
> "Sic reek as is therein maun come out at the *lum's* top."
> Proverb.

Laigh, S, low.
> "She lookit hiche to the bodynge hill,
> An' *laighe* to the darklynge deane."
> *Telfer.* The Gloamin' Bucht.

M.

Maddle, or Maffle, C, to talk or act in a silly manner.
"O, *mafflin* Gwordie, t'ou's been feulish lang."
      Graham. Gwordie and Will.

Maizelt, or Maiz't, C, stupified.
"We war fairly *maizel't* wi' t' cāld."
    Betty Yewdale. T' terrible Knitters i' Dent.
"Whyte *maiz'd* wi' loungin' on i' th' neuk."
      Stagg. Auld Lang Syne.

Maizlin, C, a simpleton.
  "Banton lads grew parfet guffs,
   An' Thursby lasses *maizlins.*"
     Mark Lonsdale. The Upshot.

Mak, C, sort, kind.
"It taks o' *maks* to mak ivery *mak.*"
    Rev. T. Clarke. Johnny Shippard.

Māp'ment, C, imbecility; compounded of mope and ment, like manage-ment, etc.
"He toked for iver sa lang, but he toked a deal o' *maapment.*"—*Ibid.*

Mattie, C, the mark at quoits or pitch and toss. *Shifting his mattie* is proverbially used for shifting position or changing policy or course.

Maukin, S, the hare.
  "The fuddlin' bodies nowadays
   Rin *maukin*-mad i' Bacchus praise."
      Ferguson. Caller Water.

Maunder, S and C, to think, talk, or act dreamily.
  "Aw wish this wanderin' wark were o'er,
   This *maunderin'* to and fro."
     Edwin Waugh. Sweetheartin' Gate.

Meat-heàl, C, very able to eat.
"He's beàth *meat-heàl* an' drink heàl. Ther' can't be mickle t' matter wid him."—Said of a Hypochondriac.

Mell, C, meddle.

"Gangin' frae house to house hearin' news an' *mellin* e ther nebbors."—*Mrs. Wheeler.* Dialogues.

Mell, S, a mallet; the prize that used to be given to the last in a race. "Winning the *Mell!*" in any contest is figuratively equivalent to taking the wooden spoon at the Cambridge examinations for honours.

Mense, S and C, propriety, creditable behaviour.
"I've seàv't beàth my meat an' my *mense.*"
Proverb, used when proffered hospitality is declined.

Messan, S and C, a small dog of indefinite breed.
"We hounds, slew the hare, quo' the bleer'd *messan.*"
Proverb.
"A little black *messet* danced sae like old Jenny."
Miss Blamire. Sec a Durdum.

Mirk, S, dark.
"It fell about the Martinmas,
 When nichts were lang an' *mirk.*"
Old Ballad—The Wife of Usher's Well.

Mischanter, S and C, misadventure.
"Thou'rt welcome, wean, *mischanter* fa' me."
Burns.

Mittens, S and C, gloves.
"He coft me a rokelay o' blue,
 An' a pair o' *mittens* o' green."
Macneil. I lo'e ne'er a laddie but ane.
"Twee yards o' red ribbon to wear for his seake,
 Forbye ledder *mittens* he bowte me."
Anderson. First Luive.

Mowdie, S; Mowdie-warp, C, the mole.
"The *mowdie* powler't oot o' the yirth,
 An' kyss't the synger's feet."
Telfer. The Gloaming Bucht.
"An' teeak us intil lile hooals under t' grūnd, ameeast like *mowdie-warps.*"—*Rev. T. Clarke.* Johnny Shippard.

Mūd, C, the past tense of must.
"He thowte 'at he *mūd* treat ye."
Miss Blamire. The Meeting.

Mutch, C, a woman's cap.
"She aff wi' her apron, put on a silk goon,
A *mutch* wi' reed ribbons, an' cam' awa' doon."
Lady Nairn. The Laird o' Cockpen.

N.

Nab, C, a promontory in a lake.
"It's o' *nabs* an' neuks is Windermer' Watter."
Said by a Coniston Man.

Neb, S and C, nose, beak.
"Gae tak this bonnie *neb* o' mine,
That picks amang the corn,
An' gi'e't to the Duke o' Hamilton,
To be a touting horn."
Old Song—Robin Redbreast's Testament.

Neàf, C, the nave of a wheel.
"T' fells spreead out fray a centre like t' spooaks of a wheel fray t' *neàf*."—A Langdale statesman.

Neif, or Neive, S and C, the hand, or fist.
"Sweet knight I kiss thy *neif*."
Shakspeare. King Henry IV.
"What's a gowpen o' glaur? It's just twa *neive* fu's o' clarts!"—*Wilson.* Noctes Ambrosianæ.

Nick't i' t' heid, C, non compos mentis.
"Toakin sike mafflement! Ye mun be *nick't i' t heead*."
A Coniston landlady to a chattering guest.

No'but, C, nothing but, only.
"He's but a simplish sooart of a body,
'At thinks there's *no'but* ya kind o' shoddy."
W. Bowness. Brough Hill Fair.

Nowte 'at dowe, C, nothing of ability, fit for nothing.
"In o' her flegmagaries donn'd
What is she?—*nowte 'at dowe!*"
Anderson. Betty Brown.

O.

Oomer, C, shade.

"Howay wi' the', an' lig down i' t' *owmer* o' t' trees till I've time ùt tak' the' afooar Mr. Machell."
Said by a farmer at Colton to an idle servant.

Oald-folk's neet, C, an assembly for feasting, dancing, and card-playing, held at the rural public houses; once, probably, confined to married people, but now open to, and attended by, young and old.

P.

Paddock rud, or rid, or ridding, C, frog-spawn.

"Auld Grizzy the witch, as some fwoke say,
Maks *paddock-rud* ointment for sair e'en."
Anderson. The Witch Wife.

Pang, C and S, to cram.

"An' some there wer could scarcely speak,
Their thropples wer sae *pang't.*"
Stagg. The Bridewain.

"It kindles wit, it waukens lair,
It *pangs* us fu' o' knowledge."
Burns. The Holy Fair.

Parlish, C, remarkable, worth speaking of.

"An' *parlish* pranks 'mang Silloth banks
They hed as they were comin'."
Stagg. The Bridewain.

"A bump as big as a young cockerel's stone,
A *parlous* knock."
Shakspeare. Romeo and Juliet.

Said to be a corruption of *perilous*, which is certainly not its meaning in Cumberland.

Pash, C, to dash or thrust down forcibly.

"Barne! I *pash't* them doon."—Said by Wm. Jackson to a neighbour's daughter after his first victory at the Flan wrestling.

Pauchtie, S, proud, supercilious.
> "*Pauchtie* damsels, bred at courts,
> Wha thraw the mou' an' tak' the dorts."
> *Ferguson.*   The Gowdspink.

Pawkie, S, sly.
> "A thief sae *pawkie* is my Jean."
> *Burns.*

Peerie, S, a peg-top. In Cumberland called a Cas'ley.
"He sleeps as soon' as onie *peerie*."—Common saying.

Phraise, C, smooth or fondling talk.
> "He's ta'en her in his armes twa,
> Wi' monie a kiss an' *phraise.*"
> Ballad—Young Huntin.

Pigs, S, pots, crockery.
> "Where the *pig's* brocken there let the sherds lie."
> Proverb.

Plack, S, the smallest coin of the old Scottish currency.
"He'll never mak his *plack* a bawbee."—Proverb.

Pleen, C, complain.
> "Thou's spoil't for o' manner o' wark,
> Thou no'but sits peghan an' *pleenan.*"
> *Mark Lonsdale.*   Love in Cumberland.

Plumb, C, (in Furness, etc., pron. Plowmb) perpendicular.

The old landlady at the boat house on Ennerdale water said of a neighbouring doctor who had visited her, and who carries his head well back, "He was mair nor *plumb!*"

Poap, C, to walk aimlessly.
> "Sūm *poapan* aboot as if they'd be hoaf dazed."
> *Rev. T. Clarke.*   T' Reysh Beearin'.

Powe, S, head, poll.
> "There's little wit within his *powe*
> That lichts a candle at the lowe."
> Proverb.

Pree, S, to taste.
> "An' aye he *preed* the lassie's mou'
> As he gaed but an' ben, O."
> Old Song.

"I *preed* her mou'." The Scotch think this phrase a poetical way of saying "I kissed her." Its literal translation into common English, "I tasted her mouth," doesn't sound like poetry; while its Cumbrian form, "I teàstit her feàce," sounds like anything rather *than* poetry; and their different versions of the same phrase illustrate rather happily the difference of character on the two sides of the Border.

Proddle, C, poke, or stir up.
> "*Proddlin'* up the smudderin' embers."
> *Stagg.*

Pubble, C, plump.
> "At Michaelmas a *pubble* goose—at Kersmas, standin' pie."
> Old Saying.

Putten down, C, put to death.
> "That nane may ken that ye are clerks,
> Till ye be *putten down.*"
> Ballad—The Clerk's Twa Sons.

Puzzen, C, poison.
> "The doctor he's a parfit plague,
> An' hauf the parish *puzzens.*"
> *Anderson.* The Village Gang.

R.

Rackups, C, a game at marbles where the loser has to place his knuckles on one side of a hole to be "fired" at with the taws of the winners. "He mun stand his *rackups*" is a proverb implying the necessity of accepting the consequences of misconduct, defeat, or miscarriage of plans.

Rakin, C, wandering far or wildly.
> "They ga *rakin* aboot widoot ayder errand or aim."
> Said of pedestrian tourists by a dalesman.

Rantin', Ranty, S and C, wild, riotous.
> "The *rantin'* dog the daidie o' t'."
> *Burns.* Song.

Ratch, C, to search vigorously, to ransack.
"*Ratch* as ye will, ye'll mak nowte out."
       Said to hunters in a wood.

Reek, S, smoke.
"The death o' deevils, smoor'd in brimstone *reek*."
       Burns. The Twa Brigs.

Riggin, S, the roof (probably from Ridging primarily).
"Ane may like the kirk weel aneuch without aye riding on the *riggin'* o' 't."—Proverb.

Rooers, C, (or rather Furness and Westmorland) oars.
"Why do you call them *rooers?*" "'Coase they irr *rooers.*" "They call them oars elsewhere." "They may co' them what they will, but if they *roo* wi' them, they're *rooers.*"
       Conversation on Esthwaite lake.

Roose, S, praise, exalt.
"*Roose* the ford as ye find it."—Proverb.

Rowp, S, auction; Rowp-crier, auctioneer.
"I canna pay't an' ye *rowp* me at the cross."
       Said by a hopeless debtor.

Rowth, S, abundance.
"Rich fouk ha'e *rowth* o' frien's."—Proverb.

Rowe, S, roll.
"Where Cart rins *rowin'* to the sea."
       Burns. The Gallant Weaver.

S.

Sackless, C, silly (originally, innocent).
"Our parson sweers a bonnie stick
  Amang thur *sackless* asses."
       Anderson. The Village Gang.

Sairy, C, sorry.
"A *sairy* wife I trowe she'd mak
 'At cudn't muck a byre."
       Ibid. Betty Brown.

Sark, C and S, shirt (male or female).
"She won't mend a *sark*, but reads novels, proud brat."
Ibid. Elizabeth's Burthday.

"Our women are nowadays a' grown sae braw,
Ilk maun ha'e a *sark*, an' some maun ha'e twa."
Ross. The wee pickle tow.

Sarra, C, serve.
"The witch wife begg'd i' our back-side,
An' went *unsarra'd* away i' the pet."
Anderson. The Witch Wife.

Sauch, S, willow.
"Whereby the glancing waves o' Clyde
Through *sauchs* an' hangin' hazels glide."
Old Song—Bothwell Bank.

Scraffle, C, scramble.
"We *scraffelt* on i' this fashion, an' it was quite dark afooar we gat till Ammelside yatt."
Betty Yewdale. T' terrible Knitters i' Dent.

Screes, C, sloping banks of fragmentary stone under precipices.
"Whoariver there's *screes*
There's mair steàns nor trees."
Old Rhymes.

Scrimp, S, pinch, reduce.
"For lack o' thee I *scrimp* my glass."
Burns. On a Bank Note.

Scrowe, S and C, a lot of children, etc. rough or numerous.
"There's sic a *scrowe* o' Irishmen come ower frae Skinburness."—Said at Annan.

Scunner, S, shuddering disgust—noun and verb.
"An' yill an' whiskey ga'e to cairds,
Until they *scunner*."
Burns. Ep. to Smith.

Sec, C ; Sic, S, such.
"Feegh ! *sec* a yen we've hed at Codbeck,
As niver was under the sun."
Anderson. The Codbeck Wedding.

"*Sic* as ye gie, *sic* will ye get."—Proverb.

Shap, C, to seem likely, or tend to.
"They're *shappin'* to gang heàm wid empty pockets."
      Said of two losing whist players at a Merry Night.

Shinny, C; Shinty, S, a rough game played with knobbed or round ended sticks—called in the south of England, I believe, hocky.
"*Shinny's* weel aneuf if shins wer' seàf."—Old saying.

Sinsyne, S, since then.
"She charm'd my heart an' aye *sinsyne*,
  I canna think o' onie ither."
        Song—O'er the Muir.

Skeich, S, shy, distant.
"Maggie coost her heid fu' heich,
Look'd asklent an' unco *skeich*."
        Burns. Duncan Gray.

Skirl, S, scream.
"White and bludy puddings rowth
To gar the doctor *skirl* wi' drowth."
        Ferguson. St. Andrews.

Skreich, S; Skrike, C, Shriek.
"It's time aneuch to *skreich* when ye're strucken."
        Proverb.

Skurl, C, slide.
"*Skurl, skurl* the' doon—I'll kep the', come thy ways,
I'll leuk ahint me—niver mind thy claes."
        Ewan Clarke.

Slake, C, a slight smear as of grease, etc.
"Let's tak' *slake* an' *slake* aboot till it's done."
      Said in licking out a treacle pot.

Slape, C, slippery.
"I mun tell her fadder when I see him—she's gittin' varra *slape*," old John Howe of Branthwaite Hall called out when he witnessed, by chance, a meeting of sweethearts on a lonely road.

Slare, C, to walk slowly.
"He may be a sharp worker, but he's a *slarin'* walker."
      Said by a farmer's wife of new come man servant.

Slashy, C, sloppy.

"It was beginnin' to thowe, an' was varra *slashy* an' cāld."
     Betty Yewdale. T' terrible Knitters i' Dent.

Slatter, C, slop.

"Wi' jaws o' yell some durty beuts
Pat loft seun in a *slatter.*"
     Mark Lonsdale. The Upshot.

Sleekie, or Sleekit, S, sly, smooth.

"O we were sly, sly!
O, we were sly an' *sleekit.*"
     Song.

Slipe, C, to slip away, to "hook it."

"*Slipe*, my lad, while thou's weel. *Slipe*, I say, an' let neàbody see the' gang."—Said to a youth in a row.

Slocken, S and C, to slake thirst.

"Ha'e ye any clippin' drink left? No! Ha'e ye any common yall? No! Ha'e ye any smo' beer? No! Why than, hang it—ha'e ye any pig-stuff? I mun be *slocken't* wi' summat!"—John Kendall at Hawkshead Hall the day after the sheep-shearing feast.

Smaik, S, a small boy, or other small animal.

"He's but a *smaik*, but he's a man at the books."
     Said of a schoolboy.

Smittal, C, infectious.

"As *smittal* as t' Smo'-pox."—Said of a successful male animal kept for breeding purposes.

Snape, C, snub, also blight.

"Yet tho' sec bruolliments galwore
Oft *snaip't* the whyet of our days."
     Stagg. Auld Lang Syne.

Sneck, C, latch.

"The Buckabank chaps are reet famous sweethearters,
Their kisses just sound like the sneck of a yett."
     Anderson. Bleckell Murry-Neet.

Sneck-posset, C. When a man has the door shut in his face, figuratively or literally, he gets a *sneck-posset.*

"Glooar'd at me a bit, an' than clyash't dewar i' mi feeace——He g'e ma a faer *sneck-possett.*"
     Rev. T. Clarke. Johnny Shippard.

Snell, S, cold and cutting.
> "There cam' a wind oot o' the north,
> A sharp wind and a *snell*."
>> Ballad—Young Tamlane.

Snirrup, or Snirp, C, to curl up the nose, etc.
> "As seun as she fund I depended on labour,
> She *snirp't* up her nose an' nae mair leuk't at me."
>> *Anderson.* The Lasses o' Carel.

Snirt, or Snurl, C, the sound of imperfectly suppressed laughter.
> "But seckan toke! nin could tell what aboot,
> I stop't my lugs for fear o' *snurtin'* oot."
>> *Graham.* Gwordie and Will.

Snod, S and C, smooth, neat.
> "Her cockermonie *snoddit* up fu' sleek,
> Her haffet locks hung wavin' owre her cheek."
>> *Ramsay.* The Gentle Shepherd.

> "You're making this road rough!" "Ey, but we'll mak it *snod* afoor we're deun wi' 't."
>> Reply of the road surveyor at Hawkshead.

Snowk, C, to snuffle audibly.
> "*Snowkin'* like pigs at a sew."—Common saying.

Snug (as a verb), C, to nestle.
> "We *snugg't* in togidder."—Ibid.

Sonsie, S, comfortable looking, also lucky.
> "Tall and *sonsie*, frank and free,
> Lo'ed by a', an' dear to me."
>> *Lady Nairne.* Kind Robin lo'es me.

> "Whistlin' maids an' crawin' hens are no *sonsie*."—Proverb.

Sorn, S, to live on others, to sponge.
> "*Sornan* frae place to place,
> As scrimp o' mainners as o' sense or grace."
>> *Ramsay.* The Gentle Shepherd.

Souch, S, the sound of gentle wind or breath.
> "Hark how the westlin' win' *souchs* through the reeds."
>> *Ibid.*

Spang-hew, S and C, to fling to the winds.

Spang-hewing is a cruel mode practised by school boys of putting birds, frogs, etc., to death. A stick is laid across a block, the victim placed on one end and the other struck sharply, throwing the poor animal high into the air, killing, and generally, mutilating it.

Spats, S and C, abbrev. of spatterdashes—gaiters.

"Their stumps, erst used to philabegs,
Are dight in *spatt*erdashes."
Ferguson. Leith Races.

Speel, S, climb.

"Monie a time,
Wi' you I've *speel'd* the braes o' rhyme."
Ferguson. My Auld Breeks.

Speir, S, ask, enquire.

"A feul may *speir* mair questions than a doctor can answer."
Proverb.

Spretty, S, covered with Sprett, a kind of coarse grass.

"Till *spretty* knowes wad rair't an' risket
An' slypet owrc."
Burns. The Auld Mare Maggie.

Sprogue, C, a pleasure ramble.

"I've been to t' top o' Knock Murton." "What took ye there?" "I just went for a *sprogue!*"

Part of a conversation in Arlecdon.

Squab, C, a long low seat with a back.

"Sit on t' *squab* till I bring ye summat to sup on."—Said to me once when I reached a farm house exhausted from struggling through a snow storm.

Stammer, or Stummer, C, to stumble.

"Oft wittingly I *stummer't*, oft I fell."
Relph. Kursty and Peggy.

'Statesman, C, landed proprietor—Estatesman.

"It is a bonnie job, if gentlemen an' gentlemen's servants is to ower-ride us *'steàts fooak.*"

Said by an old lady at Coniston after a vestry meeting.

Stayvel, or Stayver, S and C, to walk in a listless manner.

"Ther was hundreds o' fwoke *stayvelan* aboot."
Ritson. The Borrowdale Letter.

Stoore, S and C, dust.
>"This day the kirk kicks up a *stoore*."
>>Burns. The Ordination.
>"The Bible ligs *stoory* abeun the door heid."
>>Anderson. Caleb Crosby.

Stound, S and C, ache or pang.
>" An' aye the *stound*, the deidly wound,
>Cam frae her e'en sae lovely blue."
>>Burns. 'A waefu' gate yestreen.
>" It *stoundit* sare, an' sare it swell'd."
>>Relph. After Theocritus.

Straddel't, C, brought to a stand.
>"I think oald P—— was varra nār *straddel't* iv his sarmon."
>Heard at the door of a Wesleyan chapel after service.

Sumph, S and C, a fool.
>" An' onie *sumph* that keeps up spite,
>In conscience I abhor him."
>>Rev. J. Skinner. Tullochgorum.
>" I sit like a *sumph*, nea mair mysel'."
>>Anderson. Barbary Bell.

Swap, S and C, exchange.
>" I trow we *swappit* for the worse,
>Ga'e the boot an' better horse."
>>Song—Carle an the king come.
>" Lal Sim's geane an' *swapp'd* the black cowt."
>>Anderson. Nichol the Newsmonger.

Swat, C, sit down, squat.
>"Come, Cuddy, *swat* an' tak' a whiff."
>>Anderson. The Cram.

Sweir, S, loath, unwilling.
>" Forsooth they cried, anither gill,
>For *sweir* we're aye to gang awa'."
>>Mac Phail. Song.

T.

Taggelt, C, a scamp.
>"He mud know they wor o' arrant *taggelts* an' taistrels."
>>Rev. T. Clarke. Johnny Shippard.

Taistrel, C, a good for nothing.
"Yae son proved a *taistrel* an' brak up i' Lunnon."
Anderson. The Twee Auld Men.

Taws, S, a strap of thick leather slit into several tails; an implement of punishment in Scottish schools
"Never use the *taws* when a gloom 'ill do the turn."
Proverb.

Tawtie, or Tawtit, S, roughly matted (applied to hair or wool).
"Nae *tautit* tyke, though ne'er sae duddy."
Burns. The Twa Dogs.

Teem, C; Toom, S, empty, pour out.
"About her lank and all o'er *teemed* loins."
Hamlet.
"And there *toom* thy brock skin bag."
Ballad—The Fray of Suport.

Teul, C and S, a bad one (probably from devil).
"Let women deu what gud they can,
Thur wicked *teuls* 'ill lee."
Jwohnny and Jenny.

Tew, C, harass, fatigue.
"An' while they skew't an' *tew't* an' swet,
Wi' monie a weary sidle."
Mark Lonsdale. The Upshot.

Theek, S, thatch.
"An' wi' a lock o' his yellow hair,
We'll *theek* our nest when it blows bare."
Ballad—The Twa Corbies.

Thir, S; Thur, C, these.
"An' sad an' silent was the nicht
That was atween *thir* twa."
Ballad—Clark Saunders.
"*Thur* taxes! *thur* taxes! Lord help us, Amen!"
Ewan Clark. Ballad.

Thole, S, endure.
"He that has gude crops may *thole* some thistles."—Proverb.

Thowless, S and C, soft, inapt.
"Fortune aye favours the active an' bauld,
But ruins the wooer that's *thowless* an' cauld."
Ramsay. The Widow.

Threep, S and C, to aver, or argue insistingly.
> "An' fowk wad *threep* that she did green
> For what wad gar her skirl
> An' skreich some day.
>   *Ramsay.* Christ's Kirk on the Green.

> "Some *threep* 'at the times 'ill get better."
>   *Anderson.* Carel Fair.

Throssle, C, the thrush.
> "The *throssle,* when cauld winter's geane,
> Aye in our worchet welcomes spring."
>   *Anderson.* The Lass abeun Thirty.

Throughly, C, corpulent.
> "*Throughly?* ey, a gud yard through an' mair!"
> Said of Hannah Page, who sold toffy in Whitehaven.

Thyvel, C, a porridge stick.
> "She'll lick a lean *thyvel* 'at weds you."
> Said to a poor Schoolmaster at Workington.

Tine, S, lose; Tint, lost.
> "*Tine* thimble, *tine* thrift."—Proverb.

> "O have ye *tint* at tournament
> Your sword or yet your spear."
>   Ballad—The Gay Goss Hawk.

Tip, S and C, a ram.
> "She was nae get o' muirlan' *tips,*
> Wi' tawtit ket an' hairy hips."
>   *Burns.* Puir Maillie.

Tipe, C, to drink off.
> "*Tipe* it up an' hev anudder."—Common fuddling invitation.

Toozle, S and C, to rub up, to ruffle or make untidy.
> "I ance was abused i' the kirk
> For *toozling* a lass i' my daffin."
>   *Burns.* The Jolly Beggars.

Top-sark, C, an over-shirt, generally made of coarse woollen cloth.
> "We cannot bed ye o', but we can lend ye *top-sarks.*"—Said to a weather-bound party at Cockley Beck in Seathwaite.

Towp, C, capsize.
> "The leevin surs ! she *towp't* her ower
>   Or yen cud say 'Od bliss her."
> *Mark Lonsdale.* The Upshot.

Toytle, C and S, totter.
> "Tak care thou doesn't *toytle* intil t' beck."
>   Said to a top-heavy neighbour at Branthwaite.

Tryste, S, an appointed meeting, also to appoint a meeting.
> "Crack *tryste*, crack credit."—Proverb.

> "I daurna *tryste* wi' you Willie, I daurna *tryste* ye here,
>   But I'll meet wi' you in heaven Willie, i' the spring-time o'
>   the year."   *Aytoun.* Annie's Tryste.

Tyle, C, to distress, as with pain or fatigue.
> "I's *tyled* to deeth wid this kurn. I've been kurning iver sen mwornin', an' I seem as far off butter as iver."
> A farmer's wife.

U.

Unco, S ; Unket, C, strange, remarkable.
> "A hungry care's an *unco* care."—Proverb.

> "What, is there owte *unket* i' your country side?"
> *Anderson.* Bruff Reaces.

Up-bank, C, upwards.
> "Till watters run *upbank* an' trees they grow down-bank,
>   We niver can leuk on his marrow agean."
> *Anderson.* Kit Craffet.

W.

Waistrel, C, an unthrift, a useless fellow.

The late Serjeant Wilkins, in reply to the Court, once defined *waistrel* as "something spoiled in the manufacture and sold at half price in the Lowther Arcade."

Wale, S, choose, choice.
> "For sake o' gear
>   Ane *wales* a wife as he wad buy a meear."
> *Ramsay.* The Gentle Shepherd.

> "The king o' gude fellows an' *wale* o' auld men."
> Song—Auld Rob Morris.

Wankle, C, weakly, flaccid.
" As *wankle* as a wet seck."—Common saying.

Wanter, C, one wanting a wife or husband.
" He leeves aw his leane, but he's seerly to bleame,
When a *wanter* like me's to be hed sa near heame."
       Anderson. Auld Robbie Miller.

Wanwauchtie, S, unable to drink freely (wan, un, an waucht a hearty draught).
"He's unco *wanwauchtie* that scunners at whey."—Proverb.

War-day, C, work-day—so distinguished from the day of rest.
"She cheerfu' wrowte her *warday* wark,
Than sat doon at her wheel."
       Rayson. Ann o' Hethersgill.

Ware, S and C, spend.
" Jockey and Jenny they went to the fair,
Jockey gave Jenny a penny to *ware*."
       Children's Rhyme.

Wat, S, know.
"She's a wise wife that *wats* her ain weird."—Proverb.

Waukrife, S, wakeful, or preventing sleep.
" Fleas and a girnin' wife are *waukrife* bedfellows."
       Proverb.

Weird, S, fate, destiny.
" After word comes *weird*, fair fa' they that ca' me madam."
       Proverb.

Welch, C, saltless, insipid.
"What foats may poddish hev? They may be sooar, seuty, sodden, an' savvorless, soat, *welsh*, brocken, an' lumpy!"
       "Mally Bad-poddish."

Whang, C and S, a strip of leather, a piece cut off anything.
"The mergh o' his shin bane has run down on his spur leather *whang*."   The Fray of Suport.
"Wi' sweet milk cheese i' monie a *whang*."
       Burns. The Holy Fair.

Whick, C, alive, quick.
  "See fashions I'll not follow while I's *whick*,
    Lang as plain grogram and thur locks please Dick."
                    Ewan Clark.   The Faithful Pair.

Whiles, S, sometimes.
    " Wha does the utmost that he can
      May *whiles* do mair."
                    Burns.   Ep. to Dr. Blacklock.

Whins, C ; Whuns, S, furze, gorse.
  "When t' *whins* is oot o' blossom kissing's oot o' fashion."
                                                    Proverb.

Whunstane, S, a kind of hard dark stone.
      "Wha's ragin' flame an' scorchin' heat
        Wad melt the hardest *whun-stane*."
                    Burns.   The Holy Fair.

Whuddering, S and C, shuddering or tremulous in sound.
      "*Whudder* awa' thou bitter, biting blast."
                    Mactaggart.   Mary Lee's Lament.

Widderful, C, looking withered or unthriven.
  "That barne leuks as *widderful* as if it was its oan gran'-fadder."—Said of an unhealthy child.

Wimple, S, to curl and wheel as running water.
    " But I'll big a bower on yon green bank sae bonnie,
      That's laved by the waters o' Tay *wimplin'* clear."
                    Song—Bonnie Dundee.

Win, S, to make way, to get to.
  "Ye maunna think to *win* through the world on a feather bed."—Proverb.

Winnock, S, diminutive of window.
      " At yon farmer's *winnock*, nichtly,
        Still he taks his eerie stan'."
                    John Johnstone.   Bodkin Ben.

Winsome, S, winning, attractive.
      "She is a *winsome* wee thing,
        That sweet wee wife o' mine."
                    Burns.   Song.

Wizzent, C, withered, shrunk.
"He keep's a lad's heart in his *wizzent* āld skin."
                    Stanyan Bigg. Granfadder Jones.

Won, S, to exist, to dwell.
    "Kissing has *wonn'd* i' the world
    Sin ever there were twa."
                    Old Song.

Worchet, C, orchard.
    "Our meedow sud be a girt.*worchet*,
    An' growe nowte at o' but big plums."
                    Anderson. King Roger.

Wrowke, C, to disturb roughly, or stir up.
"I ola's liked John, but I cared sa lāl for Grace 'at I cūd ha' teàn her an' *wrowk't* t' fire wid her."
                    A Cumberland lady, about her children.

Wudde, S, mad.
"I've ridden a horse baith wild an' *wudde*."
                    Ballad—Kinmont Willie.

Wummel, C, to enter in a sinuous manner, as an auger bores.
"He'll *wummel* his-sel' intil t' creuktest rabbit whoal i' Siddick."—Said of a terrier.

Y.

Ya, Yan, C, one; Ae and Yin in Dumfriesshire.

Ya is used when the noun indicated is named—*yan*, when it is understood; thus—"How many fwoke was theer?" "*Yan!*" "No'but *yan*?" "No'but *ya* man!" *Ae* and *yin* are used in the same way. The use of the first is illustrated in the conversation without consonants which is said to have come off in a shop in Dumfries—Customer, referring to some cloth, asks, "A' 'oo? Shopman assents, "Ou aye a' 'oo!" Customer again, "A' *ae* 'oo?" Shopman, "Ou aye a' *ae* 'oo!" That is, "All wool?" "O yes, all wool!" "All one (or the same) wool?" "O yes, all one wool!"

Yabble, C, wealthy (literally, able).
"A varra *yabble* man i' heeh life was wantan ta simma."
                    Rev. T. Clarke. Johnny Shippard.

Yammer, S and C, to articulate quickly and indistinctly from any feeling.

"Fareweel to the bodies that *yammer* an' mourn."
Song—Bide ye yet.

"There's been a lang *yammer* in t' papers last week."
Dickinson. Scallow Beck Boggle.

Yewl, C, to weep.

"A lāl thing mak's a barne *yewl,* an' a lāl thing mak's it laugh."—Proverb.

Yoad and Yad, S and C, a mare.

"Frae Tindal-fell twelve pecks she'd bring—
She was a *yad* fit for a king."
Anderson. My bonnie black meer's deed.

Yoke, S and C, to engage with, to set to, to put a horse to a vehicle, etc.

"At length we had a hearty *yokin*
At sang about."
Burns. Ep. to Lapraik.

"An' they *yoak't* it ageàn an' laid at it wi' t' whup."
Dickinson. The Ore Carter's Wife.

Yowl, S and C, to howl.

"A dog winna *yowl* an' ye hit him wi' a bane."—Proverb.

Price 6s. Small Crown 8vo. In extra Cloth binding.

LAYS AND LEGENDS OF THE ENGLISH LAKE COUNTRY. With copious Notes. By JOHN PAGEN WHITE, F.R.C.S.

The book ought to be classic in the Lake Country.—*The Athenæum.*

These lays and legends are modern versions—and generally graceful versions—of stories that have long been current in our Lake Country. With Murray's *Handbook* for excursions, fine weather, and this volume at night in the excursionist's inn, a pleasant and profitable month may be passed in that charming district.—*Notes and Queries.*

The marks of talent are evident on every page.—*Pall Mall Gazette.*

The book is one that a tourist should be glad to find in a Lake Country inn.—*The Academy.*

A charming volume.—*The Reliquary.*

A book calculated to add much to the literary fame of Cumberland.—*Liverpool Daily Albion.*

We do not know that in our Lake Rambles, enjoyed at intervals for forty years, we ever met the gifted author, but we do know that we have rarely met with a more instructive and attractive book.—*Liverpool Mail.*

An offering to our local literature, which, for its faithfulness of colouring, only a true Cumbrian could have made.—*Carlisle Daily Journal.*

A valuable contribution to local literature.—*Carlisle Patriot.*

Certain to become a treasured book in many a Cumberland and Westmorland household.—*Whitehaven News.*

Read apart from the prose sketches, the poetical versions are gems of verse such as every true lover of poetry must appreciate.—*Kendal Mercury.*

We very cordially recommend the book.—*Wigton Advertiser.*

An excellent companion to those who desire thoroughly to enjoy the Lake District.—*Ulverston Mirror.*

We have read it through and through with great pleasure.—*Ulverston Advertiser.*

CARLISLE: G. & T. COWARD. LONDON: BEMROSE & SONS.

SECOND EDITION REVISED.

In Three Series. Price 3s. 6d. each, in Cloth binding.

THE SONGS & BALLADS OF CUMBERLAND AND THE LAKE COUNTRY; with Biographical Sketches, Notes, and Glossary. Illustrated with Portraits of Miss BLAMIRE and ROBERT ANDERSON. Edited by SIDNEY GILPIN.

FIRST SERIES contains Ancient Ballads—Cumberland Border Ballads—Rev. Josiah Relph's Songs—Miss Blamire and Miss Gilpin's Songs—Miscellaneous.

SECOND SERIES contains Songs and Ballads by Mark Lonsdale—John Stagg—Robert Anderson—John Rayson—William Wordsworth—Miscellaneous.

THIRD SERIES contains Songs and Ballads by John Woodcock Graves—John James Lonsdale—Alexander Craig Gibson—John Pagen White—John Stanyan Bigg—James Pritchett Bigg—John Richardson—Peter Burn—William Dickinson—George Dudson—Miscellaneous.

Cumberland is rich in dialect poetry and in the kind of literature that is appreciated by an intelligent peasantry. . . In the three volumes before us, Mr. Gilpin has given proof of the literary wealth to be found in that romantic region. . . The interest of some of the ballads is poetical, of others chiefly local or historical, but not one is undeserving the care bestowed upon it by the editor.—*Pall Mall Gazette.*

One of the most interesting collections of poetry which have been lately published. . . We advise the reader to buy the book, and we feel sure that he, like ourselves, will be thankful to the editor.—*Westminster Review.*

We cannot recollect a better collection.—*The Reader.*

These Cumberland lyrics—till now scattered—are on the whole well worth the pains spent on their collection.—*The Athenæum.*

It is seldom a book compiled on the local principle contains so much good matter as this collection.—*The Scotsman.*

There is much true and tender poetry in the book, and much rough, natural vigour.—*Morning Star.*

CARLISLE : G. & T. COWARD.   LONDON : BEMROSE & SONS.

Second Edition. In Cloth binding, Price 3s. 6d.
THE FOLK-SPEECH OF CUMBERLAND
and some Districts Adjacent; being short Stories and Rhymes in the Dialects of the West Border Counties. By ALEX. CRAIG GIBSON, F.S.A.

The tales are remarkable for their spirit and humour. The poetry, too, is marked by the same characteristics.—*Westminster Review.*

The stories and rhymes have the freshness of nature about them.—*Contemporary Review.*

Brimful of humour, homely wit and sense, and reflect the character and life and ways of thought of an honest sturdy people.—*Spectator.*

The stories, or prose pieces, are wonderfully clever and well done.—*Saturday Review.*

Small Crown 8vo. In neat Cloth binding, Price 3s. 6d.
"CUMMERLAND TALK;" being Short Tales and Rhymes in the Dialect of that County. By JOHN RICHARDSON, of Saint John's.

A very good specimen of its class. The ordinary subscriber to Mudie's would not for a moment dream of ever looking into it, and yet Mr. Richardson possesses far more ability than the generality of novelists who are so popular.—*Westminster Review.*

Good and pleasant.—*Saturday Review.*

There are both pathos and humour in the various stories and ballads furnished by Mr. Richardson. We congratulate Cumberland on having so many able champions and admirers of her dialect.—*Athenæum.*

CARLISLE: G. & T. COWARD. LONDON: BEMROSE & SONS.

Price 2s. 6d. Small Crown 8vo. In extra Cloth binding.

ENGLISH BORDER BALLADS.
By PETER BURN.

The Ballads are:—

The WHITE LADYE, a Tradition of Naworth Castle.
The BRIDAL O' NAWORTH,   do.   do.
MASTER WILLIAM, a Tradition of Corby Castle.
The LADYE O' BLENKINSOP, a Tradition of Blenkinsop Castle.
The GREY MAN O' BELLISTER, a Tradition of Bellister Castle.
The BONNY BAIRNS O' CAREL TOON, a Tradition of Carlisle Castle.
The GOLD TABLE O' THIRLWA', a Tradition of Thirlwall Castle.
The GOOD LADYE, a Tradition of Egremont Castle.
MAY MARYE, a Tradition of Askerton Castle.
LIZZIE BATY (The Brampton Sibyl or Witch).

And Miscellaneous Pieces.

Price 3s. 6d. in Cloth; or 5s. in Extra Gilt Binding.

POEMS. BY PETER BURN.

A NEW AND COMPLETE EDITION.

If Mr. Burn's genius does not soar very high, she leads us into many a charming scene in country and town, and imparts moral truths and homely lessons. In many points our author resembles Cowper, notably in his humour and practical aim. One end of poetry is to give pleasure, and wherever these poems find their way they will both teach and delight.—*Literary World.*

CARLISLE: G. & T. COWARD.   LONDON: BEMROSE & SONS.

www.ingramcontent.com/pod-product-compliance
Lightning Source LLC
Chambersburg PA
CBHW031826230426
43669CB00009B/1234